Davinder Kumar's

Kebabs, Chutneys & Breads

Photography & Food Styling
DHEERAJ PAUL

📖 UBSPD®
UBS Publishers' Distributors Pvt. Ltd.
New Delhi • Bangalore • Kolkata • Chennai • Patna • Bhopal • Ernakulam
Mumbai • Lucknow • Pune • Hyderabad • Bhubaneshwar • Coimbatore

UBS PUBLISHERS' DISTRIBUTORS PVT. LTD.

5 Ansari Road, **New Delhi**-110 002
Phones: 011-23273601-4, 23266646-47, 23274846, 23282281, 23273552
Fax: 23276593, 23274261• E-mail: ubspd@ubspd.com

10 First Main Road, Gandhi Nagar, **Bangalore**-560 009
Phones: 080-22253903, 22263901, 22263902, 22255153 • Fax: 22263904
E-mail: ubspd@bngm.ubspd.com, ubspdbng@airtelbroadband.in

8/1-B Chowringhee Lane, **Kolkata**-700 016
Phones: 033-22529473, 22521821, 22522910 • Fax: 22523027
E-mail: ubspdcal@cal.ubspd.com

60 Nelson Manickam Road, Aminjikarai, **Chennai**-600 029
Phones: 044-23746222, 23746351-2 • Fax: 23746287
E-mail: dbs@che.ubspd.com,ubspdche@che.ubspd.com

Ground Floor, Annapurna Complex, Naya Tola, **Patna**-800 004
Phones: 0612-2672856, 2673973, 2686170 • Fax: 2686169
E-mail: ubspdpat@pat.ubspd.com

Z-18, M.P. Nagar, Zone-I, **Bhopal**-462 011
Phones: 0755-4203183, 4203193, 2555228 • Fax: 2555285
E-mail: ubspdbhp@bhp.ubspd.com

No. 40/7940-41, Kollemparambil Chambers, Convent Road, **Ernakulam**-682 035
Phones: 0484-2353901, 2363905 • Fax: 2365511
E-mail: ubspdekm@ekm.ubspd.com

2nd Floor, Apeejay Chambers, 5 Wallace Street, Fort, **Mumbai**-400 001
Phones: 022-66376922, 66376923, 66102067, 66102069
Fax: 66376921 • E-mail: ubspdmum@mum.ubspd.com

9, Ashok Nagar, Near Pratibha Press, Gautam Buddha Marg, Latouche Road,
Lucknow-226 018 • Phones: 4025124, 4025134, 4025144, 6531753
Fax 4025144 • Email: ubspdlko@lko.ubspd.com

680 Budhwar Peth, 2nd floor, Near Appa Balwant Chowk, **Pune**-411 002
Phone: 020-24461653 • Fax: 020-24433976 • E-mail: ubspdpune@pun.ubspd.com

3rd & 4th Floors, Alekhya Jagadish Chambers, H.No.4-1-1058, Boggulkunta, Tilak Road,
Hyderabad-500 001 • Phones: 040-24754473, 24754474 • Telefax: 040-24754472
E-mail: ubspdhyd@hyd.ubspd.com

1st Floor, Plot No. 145, Cuttack Road, **Bhubaneshwar**-751 006
Phones: 0674-2314446, 2314447 • Fax: 0674-2314448
Email: ubspdbbh@bbh.ubspd.com

2nd & 3rd Floor, Sri Guru Towers, No. 1-7 Sathy Road, Cross III, Gandhipuram,
Coimbatore-641 012 • Phones: 0422-2499914, 2499916, 2499917
Fax: 0422-2499914 • Email: ubspdcbe@cbe.ubspd.com

Visit us at www.ubspd.com & www.gobookshopping.com

© **Davinder Kumar**

First Published	2002	Third Reprint	2007
First Reprint	2003	Fourth Reprint	2009
Second Reprint	2005		

ISBN 978-81-7476-389-1

Davinder Kumar asserts the moral right to be identified as the author of this work.

Photograph & Food Styling: Dheeraj Paul

Design: Ilaksha Studio Pvt. Ltd.

Printed at: International Print-O-Pac Limited, Okhla Industrial Area, Phase-I, New Delhi

▼

Davinder Kumar's
Kebabs,
Chutneys
& Breads

A
DEEP DEBT
OF
GRATITUDE

At the outset, I would like to express
my deep debt of gratitude
to the crafter of the masterpiece that is
Le Meridien today...
our late Chairman, **Charanjit Singh**—whose vision,
dedication and management skills were its building blocks.
He literally translated his vision of 'a hotel
which will shine like a jewel in the heart of the capital
and be the pride of the city' into a reality that has put **Le Meridien**
in the select class of the top hotels in the world.
It is my pleasure and privilege
to be associated with the legacy of our illustrious late Chairman
as part of the gourmets team that provides select cuisines
as hospitality of **Le Meridien,** New Delhi.

The memory of my mother who has always been a source of inspiration,
and who believed that preparing good food does not
require spices and condiments—it is the personal touch
and the way you cook that makes the food
a gourmet's delight.

ACKNOWLEDGEMENTS

▼

I am specially indebted to the following Kitchen masters
for contributing recipes and helping to perfect them:

CHEF RAJESH SHARMA
Acknowledged to be a master tandoori chef,
a reputation earned at Le Meridien, New Delhi.
Chef Sharma is the third generation of chefs coming
from a family of well-known chefs. His father,
Mr. Panna Lal Sharma is a well known chef. A graduate
from Delhi University, he has been in this profession
for the last 12 years. Over the years he has worked
in India and abroad. He is an expert in the art of
Tandoori cooking
and is called "The Kebab King".

CHEF KRISHAN SINGH NEGI
By innovating new exotic kebabs in a simple manner
Chef Negi has made Pakwan, Le Meridien's frontier
restaurant, the finest Indian restaurant. A craftsman with
15 years of experience in this profession,
he believes that the more you innovate,
the tastier will be the delicacy.

MANISH DUA
JUBY ABRAHIM
SHILPI GUPTA
GAURAV SAINI
SUSHIL JOSHI
Kitchen Team – Hotel Le Meridien

▼

A WORD ABOUT RECIPES

▼

All the **recipes** in this book have been written in a manner that makes **easy to follow**. Each recipe has been tried out personally to ensure that it is accurate and perfect.

To make preparation simple/easy, the ingredients in this book have been listed in the order in which they are to be used.

All weights are net not gross. If the recipe says 100 gms chicken it implies the weights of the ingredients after clearing and deponing. Similarly any vegetable that is required should be weighed after clearing, washing and cutting.

Each recipes yields four full portions and is sufficient to be served as a main course or single dish besides accompaniments, i.e., **salad, chutney** or **bread**. The meal is more elaborate then the full portion can be easily shared by more persons depending upon the menu.

The qualities are mentioned in **gross, tablespoon, teaspoon**, and **cups**. Each recipe has been personally tried to ensure accuracy in weight/ measures.

I have allowed our imagination free reign at times nevertheless the final product came out to be delicious and sometimes beyond expectations.

INTRODUCTION

▼

KEBABS ORIGINATED FROM TURKEY IN CENTRAL ASIA, NOW FRONTIER. KEBABS EVOLVED INTO THE FOOD OF TRUE
CONNOISSEURS IN THE KITCHEN OF AWADH. AWADH IS HOME TO A VAST VARIETY OF KEBABS.
THEY DIFFER IN SHAPE AND SIZE, THE KIND OF MEAT USED OR THE METHOD OF COOKING INVOLVED.

In Arabic the word "**KAB**" implies a turning movement. The Persian "**CABOB**" means a piece of meat or vegetable roasted or grilled on a skewer. **KAAM AAB** means with little water or semi dry. Any or all of this combined could have given rise to the word "**KEBAB**". Another reason for the increasing popularity of tandoori/charcoal grilled food in these days of healthy cuisine is that it is singularily devoid of much fat and is lighter as compared to rich curry food.

In this book I have concocted kebabs hich can be cooked in a **tandoor (clay oven)**, an open iron grill, shallow fried or deep fried or cooked on a **griddle plate (tawa)**. No doubt Tandoori Kebabs are more popular for their uniqueness. The success of a kebab depends on the succulence or freshness of tender meat, fish or vegetables, the size of course and the marination besides the right degree of cooking.

Especially in **tandoori** or **charcoal grilling**, it is an art to ensure that while cooking kebabs, the meat juices are retained.

Each preparation has its own distinguishing taste, not only because of the different texture of the meat but also because of the varying fragrances of different combinations of spices in the marination.

Whether it is the **seekh kebab**, **tandoori chicken** or **fish tikka**, or even a baby whole leg of lamb, lies the essence of mastery of tandoori cooking in the succulence of the meat and retaining the juice in a piece of dry cooked meat.

Further, when a piece of meat is plunged into a **hot tandoor** where the temperature is about **600°C**, the outer portion of the piece is roasted to a kind of a seal which keeps the juice intact inside the piece of meat when the cooking process is on at a steady **180°C**.

Indian cuisine is very rich and varied. The cuisine of the different regions of our country differs in style and content chiefly because of the use of typical spices, condiments and method of preparation.

A Few Things to Keep in Mind

- Kebabs should not be over-cooked as they tend to become dry and not remain succulent.
- Whenever Dahi (Yoghurt) is to be used for marination, it should be hung in a muslin cloth for at least 1 ½ hours before use to drain out extra whey.
- The marination should be a thick paste to coat the meat or vegetables well.
- Spices should be correctly pounded whenever possible to bring out the true flavour/aroma.
- When cream or Dahi (Yoghurt) is used, add a little refined flour or Gram flour (Besan) to prevent it from curdling.
- Remember, temperature plays an important part in Tandoori cooking. To maintain an even temperature in the tandoor, it is essential that the charcoal be evenly spread at the bottom.
- It is commonly believed that the only way to cook kebab is in a tandoor or on an open iron grill. It is true but in this book we have created several non-tandoori kebabs, shallow fried or deep fried or broiled on a griddle plate (Tawa).

▼

- For tandoori kebabs, basting acquires special significance. It is the application of butter or oil which seals in the juices and make the kebab succulent.

- Success of kebabs depends on the succulence, freshness, tenderness of meat, fish or vegetables besides the right degree of cooking.

- In tandoor or charcoal grilling, one is to ensure that while cooking kebabs, juices in meats are retained.

CONTENTS

▼

CHICKEN

▼

LAMB KEBABS

SEAFOOD

VEGETARIAN KEBABS

CHUTNEYS

ROTIS (BREADS)

COOKERY TERMS

▼

THE READER MUST FAMILIARISE HIMSELF/HERSELF WITH SOME OF THE CULINARY TERMS WHICH SPECIFICALLY LEND THIS CUISINE ITS DISTINCTIVE CHARACTER. THESE ARE DESCRIBED BELOW:

Smoking (Dhuanaar): This is a quick procedure used to flavour a meat dish. In this process smoke imparts a subtle aroma to the meat or vegetable which enhances the quality of kebab. The method is as follows. In a shallow utensil in which meat has been marinated, a small bay is made in the centre and a small bowl or onion skin is placed. A small piece of burning charcoal is placed in it and hot ghee is poured on charcoal. Sometimes mixed aromatic herbs or condiments are used for additional flavour, and immediately covered with a lid to prevent the smoke from escaping. It is left covered for about 10–15 minutes so as to allow the smoke to work on the ingredients inside. The coal is then removed from the utensils and meat put through further cooking process.

Fry: *Talna* or frying is done in a *kadai*. For kebabs use clean refined oil preferably groundnut. Use sufficient quantity of oil to ensure proper and even frying.

Baste: Moisten with fat or ghee or melted butter during roasting. For tandoori kebabs basting acquires special significance. Application of butter or oil seals in the juices and the kebabs remain succulent.

Roast: Cook in clayoven or oven.

Broil: Dry roast on griddle plate.

Grill: To cook on an open iron grill fired with charcoal.

Knead: To work a dough lightly by bringing the outside dough into the centre, using the knuckles of the hand.

Batter: A mixture of flour and liquid of such consistency that it can be used as a coating or for baking.

Bake: Cook in an oven or on a hot surface without direct exposure to a flame.

Devein: Remove the main central vein from cray fish.

INDIAN COOKERY TERMS

▼

Bharwan: Stuffed.

Tikka: Small chunks of meat, chicken or fish, usually chicken, which can be skewered before roasting in the tandoor.

Kebab: Fish, chicken lamb or vegetable, usually skewered (whole cubes or mince) and roasted in a tandoor or grilled on charcoal iron grill. Also shallow fried on a griddle plate (e.g. Galouti, Shammi, etc.).

Marination: To soak meat, fish, vegetable before cooking in a mixture with spices, oil, yoghurt, cream to ensure that spices, herbs penetrate into the food item for flavour.

Marinade: Mixture in which spices, herbs, oil, yoghurt, cream, egg, as per choice have been mixed together for marination of meat, fish or vegetables.

Masala: In marination of kebabs one uses different kinds of masalas such as Garam masala, Tandoori masala, etc. These have been listed separately on page 195.

Galavat: Refers to the use of softening agents such as PAPAIN (Raw Papaya), or Kalmi Shora to tenderise meat.

WEIGHTS AND MEASURES

▼

Weight Equivalents

Ounces	Grams
½ oz	14 gm
1 oz	28 gm
2 oz	57 gm
3 oz	85 gm
4 oz (¼ B)	113 gm
5 oz	142 gm
6 oz	170 gm
7 oz	198 gm
8 oz (½ B)	227 gm
9 oz	255 gm
10 oz	284 gm
11 oz	312 gm
12 oz (¾ B)	340 gm
13 oz	369 gm
14 oz	397 gm
15 oz	425 gm
16 oz (1 lb)	454 gm
24 oz	680 gm
32 oz (2 lb)	908 gm

Liquid Measures Equivalents

Liquid Measures	Cup Measures	Liquid Measures
1 fl oz		30 ml
2 fl oz	¼ cup	60 ml
3 fl oz		100 ml
4 fl oz	½ cup	125 ml
5 fl oz		150 ml
6 fl oz	3/4 cup	185 ml
8 fl oz	1 cup	240 ml
10 fl oz (½ pt.)	1¼ cups	

Ounces	Grams
1 tsp	= 5 gm
2 tsp	= 10 gm
3 tsp	= 15 gm = 1 tbsp = ½ fl oz

Chicken

▼

POULTRY

Poultry is a misunderstood word; many people associate only chicken with poultry. No doubt, chicken is more universal and in India it certainly is the most popular bird, but many other varieties of birds that come under poultry are eaten all over the world.

Other types of poultry commonly used in tandoori cuisine are Partridge (teetar) and Quail (bater). These are rare delicacies.

An important consideration in choosing chicken for kebabs will vary on the type of kebab to be made.

Whole Chicken : Use small birds (skinless)
Weight approx 650–700 gms
(ideal for tandoori chicken)

Large Pieces on Bone : Use medium sized broiler (skinless)
Weight approx 750–850 gms
4 in number, i.e., 2 breast and 2 legs.
8 in number, i.e., 4 each of breast and leg
(ideal for banquet menus)

Boneless : Use large broilers (skinless)
Weight approx 1000–1250 gms
2-inch pieces from the leg and breast

Mince : Use large broilers (skinless)
Finely minced

▼

Ingredients

Chicken breast (boneless)	-	850 gm
Ginger garlic paste	-	30 gm
Lemon juice	-	25 ml
Salt	-	to taste
Yellow chilly powder	-	15 gm
Garam masala	-	5 gm
Chana dal	-	250 gm
Hung curd	-	300 ml
Cream	-	150 ml
Nutmeg powder	-	pinch
Refined oil	-	80 ml
Melted butter	-	for basting

Method

Clean, wash and cut each chicken breast into two and pat dry.

First Marination

1. Apply ginger garlic paste, lemon juice, salt yellow chilli powder and garam masala, rub well and leave aside for 1 hour.

2. Soak chana dal overnight, drain water. In a blender, make a fine paste and transfer it to a bowl.

Second Marination

1. In a bowl whisk hung curd, add chana dal paste, cream, nutmeg and refined oil, and mix well.

2. After squeezing out the excess moisture, put the marinated chicken pieces into this marinade. Rub the chicken pieces well and keep aside for 2-3 hours.

Cooking

1. Take a skewer and skew the marinated chicken pieces, keep a tray underneath to collect drippings.

2. Roast in a moderately hot tandoor or over a charcoal grill for 6-7 minutes.

3. Remove and hang the skewer to let excess moisture drain out completely (2-3 minutes). Baste with melted butter and roast for another 3-4 minutes.

4. Transfer cooked chicken on to a plate.

5. Serve hot with choice of salad and chutney.

TO SERVE: 4

COOKING TIME: 8–10 Minutes

MURG JEERA TIKKA

▼

Ingredients

Chicken leg (boneless)	-	850 gm
Hung curd	-	200 gm
Ginger garlic paste	-	2 tbsp
Brown onion paste	-	1 tbsp
Shahi jeera	-	2 tsp
Roasted cumin powder	-	4 tbsp
Kashmiri red chilli powder	-	2 tsp
Black salt	-	1 tsp
Refined oil	-	80 ml
Salt	-	to taste
Melted butter	-	for basting

Method

Clean, wash and cut each leg into 4 pieces, pat dry and keep aside.

Marination

1. In a bowl whisk hung curd, add ginger garlic paste, brown onion paste, shahi jeera and the remaining ingredients in the order listed. Adjust seasoning.

2. Put chicken pieces in this mixture and rub well. Keep aside for 3 hours.

Cooking

1. Take a skewer and skew the marinated chicken pieces, keep a tray underneath to collect drippings.

2. Roast in a moderately hot tandoor or over a charcoal grill for 6-7 minutes.

3. Remove and hang the skewer to let excess moisture drain out completely (2-3 minutes). Baste with melted butter and roast for another 3-4 minutes.

4. Transfer chicken on to a plate.

5. Serve hot with choice of salad and chutney.

TO SERVE: 4

COOKING TIME: 10–12 Minutes

MURG SAUNFIYA TIKKA

▼

Ingredients

Boneless chicken breast	-	8 nos.
Hung curd	-	300 gm
Cream	-	20 ml
Ginger garlic paste	-	1 tbsp
Egg	-	1 no.
Salt	-	to taste
Kashmiri red chilli powder	-	3 tbsp
Garam masala powder	-	½ tsp
Aniseed powder	-	4 tbsp
Cornflour	-	1 tbsp
White vinegar	-	1 tsp
Refined oil	-	80 ml
Melted butter	-	for basting

Method
Clean the chicken breasts and cut each into two pieces breadthwise and pat dry with a cloth.

Marination
In a bowl whisk hung curd, cream, ginger garlic paste, egg and remaining ingredients in the order listed. Dip chicken pieces and rub thoroughly with the mixture and keep aside for 3-4 hours.

Cooking
1. Take a skewer and skew the marinated chicken pieces, keep a tray underneath to collect drippings.

2. Roast in a moderately hot tandoor or over a charcoal grill for 6-7 minutes.

3. Remove and hang the skewer to let excess moisture drain out completely (2-3 minutes). Baste with melt butter and roast for another 3-4 minutes.

4. When cooked transfer chicken on to a plate.

5. Serve hot with choice of salad and chutney.

TO SERVE: 4

COOKING TIME: 8-10 Minutes

▼

Ingredients

Chicken breast (boneless)	-	850 gm
Hung curd	-	300 ml
Rose leaves powder (Rani masala)	-	50 gm
Shahi jeera	-	1 tsp
Ginger garlic paste	-	2 tbsp
Sesame seed paste	-	3 tbsp
Cashewnut paste	-	3 tbsp
Garam masala	-	1 tsp
Kashmiri red chilli powder	-	3 tsp
White vinegar	-	3 tsp
Rose water	-	4 tsp
Refined oil	-	90 ml
Egg	-	1 no.
Salt	-	to taste
Melted butter	-	for basting

TO SERVE: 4

COOKING TIME: 8-10 Minutes

Method

Clean, wash and cut each chicken breast into half and pat dry with a cloth.

Marination

1. In a deep tray whisk hung curd, add rose leaves powder, shahi jeera, ginger ginger garlic paste, sesame seed paste and cashewnut paste. Sprinkle garam masala, kashmiri red chilli powder, white vinegar, rose water, refined oil, egg and adjust salt and mix well.

2. Put chicken pieces in this mixture and rub well. Keep aside for 2 hours.

Cooking

1. Take a skewer and skew the marinated chicken pieces, keep a tray underneath to collect drippings.

2. Roast in a moderately hot tandoor or over a charcoal grill for 5-6 minutes.

3. Remove and hang the skewer to let excess moisture drain out completely (2-3 minutes). Baste with melted butter and roast for another 3-4 minutes.

4. Transfer chicken on to a plate when cooked.

5. Serve hot with choice of salad and chutney.

▼

Ingredients

Chicken breast (boneless)	-	850 gm
Ginger garlic paste	-	2 tbsp
Salt	-	to taste
White pepper powder	-	1 tbsp
Shahi jeera	-	½ tbsp
Refined oil	-	10 ml
Grated processed cheese	-	200 gm
Egg white	-	1 no.
Cream	-	400 ml
Elaichi javitri powder	-	½ tbsp
Chopped green chilli	-	5 gm
Chopped coriander roots	-	5 gm
Melted butter	-	for basting

Method

Clean, wash chicken breasts and flatten with steak hammer, pat dry.

First Marination

Apply ginger garlic paste, salt half of white pepper powder, shahi jeera and refined oil to the chicken pieces and rub well. Keep aside for 1 hour.

Second Marination

1. In a deep tray put grated cheese, egg white and mix gradually with your palm. Pour cream and further mix so that it becomes a smooth paste. Add salt remaining white pepper powder, elaichi javitri powder, chopped green chilli, chopped coriander roots and mix well.

2. Put marinated chicken pieces into this marinade after removing the excess moisture. Rub well along with the marinade and keep aside for 2 hours.

Cooking

1. Take a skewer and skew the marinated chicken pieces, keep a tray underneath to collect drippings.

2. Roast in a moderately hot tandoor or over a charcoal grill for 6-7 minutes.

3. Remove and hang the skewer to let excess moisture drain out completely (2-3 minutes). Baste with melted butter and roast for another 3-4 minutes.

4. Transfer chicken on to a plate when cooked.

5. Serve hot with choice of salad and chutney.

TO SERVE: 4

COOKING TIME: 10-12 Minutes

▼

Ingredients

Chicken mince	-	800 gms
Processed cheese	-	100 gms
Cream	-	100 gms
Ginger garlic paste	-	10 gms
Red chilli powder	-	5 gms
Javitri powder	-	1 gms
Chhoti elachi powder	-	2 gms
Kebab chini powder	-	2 gms
Itre (essence)	-	1 drop
Corriender (chopped)	-	10 gms
Green chilli (chopped)	-	5 gms
Salt	-	to taste
Chandi ki verk (silver leaves)	-	16 nos.
Refined oil	-	for frying

Method

1. Grate processed cheese in a bowl/paraat. Pour cream gradually and mix untill it gets blended and smooth.

2. Take chicken mince, add cheese and cream mixture, ginger garlic paste, red chilli powder, and all other ingredients in the order listed.

3. Mix throughly until smooth.

4. Divide mixture into 16 equal portions and make round balls each of 50 gms.

5. Slightly flatten the balls and roll over silver leaves (verk) so it gets evenly covered from all sides.

Cooking

1. Heat oil in a deep bottomed pan. Fry these balls in medium heat until they get cooked.

2. Remove and strain excess oil.

3. Serve hot along with choice of salad and chutney.

TO SERVE: 4

COOKING TIME: 8-10 Minutes

▼

Ingredients

Chicken fillets	-	800 gm
Kasoori methi powder	-	2 tbsp
Ginger garlic paste	-	4 tbsp
Saffron	-	2 pinch
Egg yolk	-	8 no.
Garam masala powder	-	1 tsp
Kashmiri red chilli powder	-	3 tsp
Turmeric powder	-	1 tsp
Refined oil	-	100 ml
Lemon juice	-	50 ml
Salt	-	to taste
Melted butter	-	for basting

Method

Clean the chicken fillets, sprinkle kasoori meethi powder and mix well. Keep aside.

Marination

1. In a bowl put ginger garlic paste, saffron, egg yolk, garam masala, kashmiri red chilli powder, turmeric powder, refined oil, lemon juice and salt. Mix well.

2. Put chicken fillets in the above marinade and rub well. Keep aside for 2-3 hours.

Cooking

1. Take a skewer and skew the marinated chicken pieces, keep a tray underneath to collect drippings.

2. Roast in a moderately hot tandoor or over charcoal grill for 2-3 minutes.

3. Remove and hang the skewer to let excess moisture drain out completely (2-3 minutes). Baste with melted butter and roast for another 2-3 minutes.

4. Transfer chicken on to a plate.

5. Serve hot with choice of salad and chutney.

TO SERVE: 4

COOKING TIME: 5-6 Minutes

▼

▼

Ingredients

Chicken leg (boneless)	-	850 gm
Hung curd	-	300 gm
Ginger garlic paste	-	1 tbsp
Green chilly paste	-	1 tsp
Red chilly powder	-	2 tbsp
Red chilly paste	-	2 tbsp
Kebab chini powder	-	¼ tsp
Chaat masala powder	-	1 tbsp
Salt	-	to taste
Cornflour	-	2 tbsp
Lemon juice	-	1 tbsp
Refined oil	-	80 ml

Method

Clean, wash and cut the chicken leg into four pieces each and pat dry with a cloth and keep aside.

Marination

1. In a bowl whisk hung curd and add the remaining ingredients in the order listed. Red chilly can be adjusted according to taste.

2. Put the chicekn pieces into the marinade, a rub well and keep aside for 2-3 hours.

Cooking

1. Take a skewer and skew the marinated chicken pieces, keeping a tray underneath to collect drippings.

2. Roast in a moderately hot tandoor or over a charcoal grill for 6-7 minutes, until half done.

3. Remove and hang the skewer to let excess moisture drip (2-3 minutes). Baste with clarified butter and roast for another 3-4 minutes.

4. When cooked transfer chicken on to a plate.

5. Serve hot with choice of salad and chutney.

TO SERVE: 4

COOKING TIME: 10-12 Minutes

▼

Ingredients

Chicken leg (boneless)	-	850 gm
Hung curd	-	300 ml
Cream	-	300 ml
Garlic paste	-	20 gm
English mustard paste	-	100 gm
Egg yolk	-	I no.
Chopped garlic	-	25 gm
Chopped curry leaves	-	10 gm
Salt	-	to taste
Kashmiri red chilli powder	-	2 tbsp
Garam masala	-	I tsp
Turmeric powder	-	a pinch
Roasted semolina	-	25 gm
Saffron	-	2 pinch
Cornflour	-	10 gm
Lemon juice	-	30 ml
Refined oil	-	80 ml
Melted butter	-	For basting

Method

Clean, wash and cut each chicken leg into 4 pieces and pat dry with a cloth.

Marination

1. In a bowl whisk hung curd, add the remaining ingredients in the order listed and mix.

2. Rub the chicken pieces with this mixture and keep aside for 2-3 hours.

Cooking

1. Take a skewer and skew the marinated chicken pieces, keep a tray underneath to collect drippings.

2. Roast in a moderately hot tandoor or over charcoal grill for 6-7 minutes.

3. Remove and hang the skewer to let excess moisture drain out completely (2-3 minutes). Baste with melted butter and roast for another 3-4 minutes.

4. Transfer cooked chicken on to a plate.

5. Serve hot with choice of salad and chutney.

TO SERVE: 4

COOKING TIME: 10-12 Minutes

LAHSUNI MURG TIKKA

▼

Ingredients

Chicken leg (boneless)	-	850 gm
Garlic paste	-	50 gm
Lemon juice	-	10 ml
Salt	-	to taste
Yellow chilli powder	-	1½ tbsp
Gram flour (roasted)	-	100 gm
Refined oil	-	200 ml
Melted butter	-	for basting

Method

Clean, wash and cut each chicken leg into 4 pieces and pat dry with a cloth.

Marination

1. Apply garlic paste, lemon juice, yellow chilli powder and salt and keep aside for 1 hour.

2. In a tray take marinated chicken add gram flour and mix well.

3. Pour refined oil and further mix so that oil gets blended easily. Add all the remaining ingredients and mix well.

Cooking

1. Take a skewer and skew the marinated chicken pieces, keep a tray underneath to collect drippings.

2. Roast in a moderately hot tandoor or over a charcoal grill for 6-7 minutes, until half done.

3. Remove and hang the skewer to let excess moisture drain out completely (2-3 minutes). Baste with melted butter and roast for another 3-4 minutes.

4. Transfer cooked chicken on to a plate.

5. Serve hot with choice of salad and chutney.

TO SERVE: 4

COOKING TIME: 12-15 Minutes

MURG KHATTA MEETHA

▼

Ingredients

Chicken leg (boneless)	-	850 gm
Ginger garlic paste	-	1 tbsp
Lemon juice	-	30 ml
Salt	-	to taste
Aampapad	-	300 gm
Green chilli	-	10 gm
Coriander leaves	-	10 gm
Curry leaves	-	10 gm
Hung curd	-	250 gm
Kashmiri red chilli powder	-	1 tbsp
Garam masala	-	1 tbsp
Groundnut oil	-	90 ml
Peanut paste	-	1 tbsp
Melted butter	-	for basting

Method

Clean, wash and cut each chicken leg into 4 pieces and pat dry with a cloth.

First Marination

Apply ginger garlic paste, lemon juice and salt to the chicken and keep aside for 1 hour.

Second Marination

1. Soak the aampapad in a little warm water. Put this in a blender along with green chillies, coriander and curry leaves to make a paste.

2. In a bowl, whisk hung curd, add red chilli powder, garam masala, groundnut oil. Add the above made paste, peanut paste and mix well. Adjust salt to taste.

3. Remove the excess moisture from the marinated chicken, mix well with the second marination and leave aside for 2-3 hours.

Cooking

1. Take a skewer and skew the marinated chicken pieces. Keep a tray underneath to collect drippings.

2. Roast in a moderately hot tandoor or over a charcoal grill for 6-7 minutes.

3. Remove and hang the skewer to let excess moisture drain out completely (2-3 minutes). Baste with clarified butter and roast for another 3-4 minutes.

4. Transfer cooked chicken on to a plate.

5. Serve hot with choice of salad and chutney.

TO SERVE: 4

COOKING TIME: 10-12 Minutes

▼

Ingredients

Chicken leg (boneless)	-	850 gm
Apples (cooking)	-	6 nos.
Cashewnut paste	-	5 tbsp
Green chilli paste	-	1 tbsp
Hung curd	-	350 gm
Cream	-	200 ml
Rose water	-	½ tsp
Kewra water	-	½ tsp
Egg	-	2 nos.
Refined flour	-	2 tsp
Cornflour	-	2 tsp
Malt vinegar	-	2 tbsp
White vinegar	-	3 tbsp
White pepper powder	-	1 tsp
Elaichi powder	-	2 tsp
Refined oil	-	80 ml
Ginger garlic paste	-	4 tbsp
Rose petal powder	-	2 tbsp
Salt	-	to taste
Melted butter	-	for basting

Method

1. Clean, wash and cut each chicken leg into 4 pieces and pat dry with a cloth.

2. Peel, cut, deseed apples and make a puree in a blender.

Marination

1. In a bowl take cashewnut paste, green chilly paste, hung curd, and cream and add the remaining ingredients in the order listed. Mix well.

2. Put chicken pieces in this marinade, rub well and keep aside for 2 hours.

Cooking

1. Take a skewer and skew the marinated chicken pieces. Keep a tray underneath to collect drippings.

2. Roast in a moderately hot tandoor or over a charcoal grill for 6-7 minutes.

3. Remove and hang the skewer to let excess moisture drain out completely (2-3 minutes). Baste with melted butter and roast for another 4-5 minutes.

4. Transfer cooked chicken on to a plate.

5. Serve hot with choice of salad and chutney.

TO SERVE: 4

COOKING TIME: 10-12 Minutes

ACHARI MURG TIKKA

▼

Ingredients

Chicken leg (boneless)	-	850 gm
Ginger garlic paste	-	2 tbsp
Salt	-	to taste
Lemon juice	-	30 ml
Hung curd	-	300 gm
Roasted gram flour	-	3 tbsp
Achari paste	-	150 gm
Kalonji seed		1 tsp
Black salt	-	1 tsp
Turmeric powder	-	1 tsp
Mustard oil	-	80 ml
Junglee masala	-	2 tbsp
Malt vinegar	-	1 tbsp
Melted butter	-	for basting

Method

Clean, wash and cut each chicken leg into 4 pieces and pat dry with a cloth.

First Marination

Apply ginger garlic paste, lemon juice and salt to chicken pieces. Rub well and keep aside for 1 hour.

Second Marination

1. In a bowl, whisk hung curd, and add the remaining ingredients in the order listed. Add salt as per taste and mix well.

2. Remove excess moisture from the chicken pieces and mix along with the second marinade, rub well and leave aside for 2 hours.

Cooking

1. Take a skewer and skew the marinated chicken pieces. Keep a tray underneath to collect drippings.

2. Roast in a moderately hot tandoor or over a charcoal grill for 6-7 minutes.

3. Remove and hang the skewer to let excess moisture drain out completely (2-3 minutes). Baste with meltedbutter and roast for another 3-4 minutes.

4. Transfer cooked chicken on to a plate.

5. Serve hot with choice of salad and chutney.

TO SERVE: 4

COOKING TIME: 10-12 Minutes

MURG BANJARA TIKKA

▼

Ingredients

Chicken leg (boneless)	-	850 gm
Ginger garlic paste	-	1 tbsp
Lemon juice	-	2 tbsp
Salt	-	to taste
Hung curd	-	250 gm
Roasted peanut paste	-	125 gm
Dry mango powder	-	1 tsp
Red chilli powder	-	2 tbsp
Coriander paste	-	2 tbsp
Junglee masala	-	4 tbsp
Mustard oil	-	80 ml
Vinegar	-	1 tbsp
Melted butter	-	for basting

TO SERVE: 4

COOKING TIME: 10-12 Minutes

Method

Clean, wash and cut each chicken leg into 4 pieces and pat dry with a cloth.

First Marination

Apply ginger garlic paste, lemon juice, and salt and leave aside for 1 hour.

Second Marination

1. In a bowl, whisk hung curd and add the remaining ingredients in the order listed. Mix well and adjust salt to taste.

2. Put marinated chicken pieces into above marinade after squeezing the excess moisture. Rub the chicken pieces well with the above mixture and keep aside for 2-3 hours.

Cooking

1. Take a skewer and skew the marinated chicken pieces. Keep a tray underneath to collect drippings.

2. Roast in a moderately hot tandoor or over a charcoal grill for 6-7 minutes.

3. Remove and hang the skewer to let excess moisture drain out completely (2-3 minutes). Baste with melted butter and roast for another 3-4 minutes.

4. Transfer when cooked chicken on to a plate.

5. Serve hot with choice of salad and chutney.

POTLI KEBAB

▼

Ingredients

Chicken breast boneless	-	8 nos.

Stuffing

Refined oil	-	50 ml
Shahi jeera	-	1 tsp
Elaichi (seeds only)	-	7 nos.
Onion (chopped)	-	50 gm
Ginger (chopped)	-	10 gm
Green chilli (chopped)	-	10 gm
Chicken mince	-	250 gm
Coriander leaves (chopped)	-	10 gm
Dry kasoori methi powder	-	1 tsp
Chaat masala	-	1 tsp
Elaichi javitri powder	-	½ tsp
Mixed dry fruits (chopped)	-	100 gm
Salt	-	to taste

Marination

Hung curd	-	400 gm
Cream	-	200 ml
Ginger garlic paste	-	2 tbsp
Cashewnut paste	-	3 tbsp
Green chilli paste	-	1 tbsp
Grated cheese	-	50 gm
Egg yolk	-	2 nos.
Salt	-	to taste
Elaichi javitri powder	-	1 tsp
White pepper powder	-	1 tsp
Kasoori methi	-	1 tsp
Refined oil	-	80 ml
Cornflour	-	2 tsp
Melted butter	-	for basting

TO SERVE: 4

COOKING TIME: 12-15 Minutes

Method

Clean each chicken breast of excess fat. Slit half way through the centre on the inside and open the breast. Flatten lightly with a steak bat. Keep aside.

Stuffing

Heat oil in a pan, add shahi jeera and elaichi seeds. Sauté chopped onions in the oil, add ginger and green chilli. Sauté. Add the chicken mince and cook. When cooked add chopped coriander, kasoori methi, chaat masala and elaichi javitri powder along with the chopped mixed dry fruits. Season and let it cool.

Marination

1. In a bowl take hung curd and all the remaining ingredients for marination. Mix and keep aside.
2. When the stuffing is cooled, make equal balls and place each ball on the flattened chicken breast. Close the breast around the ball in the shape of a potli and tie it with a thread.
3. Dip the potli in the marinade and keep under refrigeration for 2-3 hours.

Cooking

1. Take a skewer and skew the chicken breast horizontally, leaving a gap of at least an inch between the breasts.
2. Roast in a moderately hot tandoor for 8-10 minutes. Remove and hang so that the excees moisture drains out completely.
3. Baste with melted butter and roast further for 3-4 minutes.
4. Transfer on to the plate, remove the thread and serve hot with choice of salad and chutney.

TANDOORI BHARWAN TANGRI

TANDOORI BHARWAN TANGRI

▼

Ingredients

Chicken drumsticks	-	16 nos.

Stuffing

Butter	-	30 gm
Roasted cashewnut	-	20 gm
Chicken mince	-	400 gm
Salt	-	to taste
Yellow chilly powder	-	1 tsp
Garam masala	-	1 tsp
Green chilly (chopped)	-	10 gm
Coriander (chopped)	-	20 gm
Saffron	-	a pinch

First Marination

Ginger garlic paste	-	1 tbsp
Lemon juice	-	10 ml
White pepper powder	-	1 tsp
Salt	-	to taste

Second Marination

Grated processed cheese	-	200 gm
Egg white	-	1 no.
Cream	-	500 ml
Ginger garlic paste	-	1 tsp
Salt	-	to taste
White pepper powder	-	1 tbsp
Elaichi javitri powder	-	½ tsp
Green chilli (chopped)	-	5 mg
Coriander roots (chopped)	-	5 gm
Melted butter	-	for basting

TO SERVE: 4

COOKING TIME: 15-20 Minutes

Method

1. Clean, wash the chicken legs and pat dry. Keep aside.
2. With a knife tip make a deep slit along the bone.

Stuffing

1. Heat butter in a pan, add roasted cashew nuts, chicken mince and saute until meat turns white. Add salt, yellow chilli powder, garam masala, chopped green chilli, coriander and saffron. Cook until moisture evaporates and the mixture becomes completely dry.
2. Remove from fire and cool.
3. Divide this mixture into 16 equal portions and stuff each tangri with this mixture.
4. Give three incisions on the back side of the tangri.

First Marination

Apply ginger garlic paste, lemon juice, salt, white pepper powder and keep aside for 1 hour.

Second Marination

1. In a deep tray, put grated cheese, egg white and mix with the palm gradually. Pour cream and further mix so that it becomes a smooth paste. Add the remaining ingredients and mix.
2. Put marinated chicken into this mixture. Rub well along with the marinade and keep aside for 2-3 hours.

Cooking

1. Take a skewer and skew chicken legs horizontally, leaving a gap of at least an inch between each leg.
2. Roast in a moderately hot tandoor or over a charcoal grill for 10-12 minutes. Removed and hang so that the excess moisture drain out completely..
3. Baste with melted butter and roast again for 3-4 minutes.
4. Serve hot with choice of salad and chutney.

▼

MURG NASHEELA TIKKA

▼

Ingredients

Chicken leg (boneless)	-	850 gm
Refined oil	-	3 tbsp
Butter (softened)	-	2 tbsp
Refined flour	-	3 tbsp
Cornflour	-	2 tbsp
Rum	-	120 ml
Ginger (chopped)	-	1 tbsp
Garlic (chopped)	-	1 tbsp
Green chilli (chopped)	-	½ tbsp
Coriander (chopped)	-	2 tbsp
Red chilli powder	-	1 tbsp
Cumin powder	-	1 tsp
Clove powder	-	1 tsp
Crushed pepper corn	-	1 tsp
Lemon juice	-	2 tbsp
Malt vinegar	-	2 tbsp
Salt	-	to taste
Melted butter	-	for basting

TO SERVE: 4

COOKING TIME: 10-12 Minutes

Method

Clean, wash and cut each chicken leg into 4 pieces, pat dry and keep aside.

Marination

1. In a pan, heat refined oil and butter, add refined flour, cornflour and cook for a while. Remove from the fire and add 120 ml of rum. Keep aside to cool. Transfer to a bowl, add the remaining ingredients into the mixture in the order listed and mix well.

2. Mix the chicken pieces into the marinade, rub well and keep aside for 2-3 hours.

Cooking

1. Take a skewer and skew the marinated chicken pieces, keep a tray underneath to collect drippings.

2. Roast in a moderately hot tandoor or over a charcoal grill for 6-7 minutes, until half done.

3. Remove and hang the skewer to let excess moisture drain out completely (2-3 minutes). Baste with melted butter and roast for another 3-4 minutes.

4. Transfer chicken when cooked on to a plate.

5. Serve hot with choice of salad and chutney.

MURG CHOPATTI TIKKA

▼

Ingredients

Chicken leg (boneless)	-	850 gm
Refined oil	-	30 ml
Garlic (chopped)	-	60 gm
Garlic paste	-	50 gm
Curry powder	-	2 tbsp
Red chilli paste	-	6 tbsp
Vinegar	-	4 tbsp
Hung curd	-	300 gm
Garam masala	-	¼ tbsp
Tandoori masala	-	½ tbsp
Cornflour	-	1 tbsp
Lemon juice	-	3 tbsp
Salt	-	to taste
Melted butter	-	for basting

Method

1. Clean, wash and cut each chicken leg into 4 pieces and pat dry with a cloth.

2. In a pan heat 30 ml refined oil, add chopped garlic, garlic paste, curry powder, chilli paste and cook for a while adding vinegar to it. Keep aside to cool.

Marination

1. In a bowl whisk hung curd, add the above mixture, garam masala, tandoori masala, cornflour, lemon juice, and salt as per taste. Mix well.

2. Put the chicken pieces into this marinade, rub well and keep aside for 2-3 hours.

Cooking

1. Take a skewer and skew the marinated chicken pieces, keep a tray underneath to collect drippings.

2. Roast in a moderately hot tandoor or over a charcoal grill for 6-7 minutes, until half done.

3. Remove and hang the skewer to let excess moisture drain out completely (2-3 minutes). Baste with melted butter and roast for another 3-4 minutes.

4. Transfer chicken when cooked on to a plate.

5. Serve hot with choice of salad and chutney.

TO SERVE: 4

COOKING TIME: 10-12 Minutes

ROGANI MURG TIKKA

▼

Ingredients

Chicken leg (boneless)	-	850 gm
Refined oil	-	1 tsp
Curry leaves	-	5 gm
Hung yoghurt	-	300 ml
Garlic (chopped)	-	10 gm
Onions (chopped)	-	15 gm
Ginger (chopped)	-	10 gm
Green chilli (chopped)	-	5 gm
Salt	-	to taste
Red chilli powder	-	1 tbsp
Garam masala	-	1 tbsp
Lemon juice	-	20 ml
Rogan	-	120 ml
Melted butter	-	for basting

Method

1. Clean, wash and cut each chicken leg into 4 pieces and pat dry with a cloth.

2. In a pan heat the refined oil and fry curry leaves until they crackle. Keep aside.

Marination

1. In a bowl whisk hung curd, add fried curry leaves and the remaining ingredients in the order listed. Mix well.

2. Put chicken pieces into this marinade and rub well. Keep aside for 1½-2 hours.

Cooking

1. Take a skewer and skew the marinated chicken pieces. Keep a tray underneath to collect drippings.

2. Roast in a moderately hot tandoor or over a charcoal grill for 6-7 minutes, until half done.

3. Remove and hang the skewer to let excess moisture drain out completely (2-3 minutes). Baste with melted butter and roast for another 3-4 minutes.

4. Transfer chicken when cooked on to a plate.

5. Serve hot with choice of salad and chutney.

TO SERVE: 4

COOKING TIME: 10-12 Minutes

MURG JAHANGIRI TIKKA

▼

Ingredients

Chicken leg (boneless)	-	850 gm
Mustard oil	-	100 ml
Cumin seed	-	5 gm
Ginger (chopped)	-	50 gm
Green chilli (chopped)	-	30 gm
Green coriander (chopped)	-	100 gm
Asafoetida water	-	50 ml
Hung curd	-	300 ml
Grated processed cheese	-	20 gm
Ginger (chopped)	-	5 gm
Coriander leaves (chopped)	-	15 gm
Salt	-	to taste
White pepper powder	-	½ tsp
Crushed black pepper	-	2 tbsp
Black salt	-	1 tbsp
Raw mango powder	-	1 tbsp
Cornflour	-	20 gm
Lemon juice	-	80 ml
Mustard oil	-	50 ml
Melted butter	-	for basting

TO SERVE: 4

COOKING TIME: 10-12 Minutes

Method

1. Clean, wash and cut each chicken leg into 4 pieces. Pat dry with a cloth.

2. Heat mustard oil in a pan, add cumin seeds, chopped ginger, green chillies and coriander leaves. Sauté for some time.

3. Add asafoetida water to it, remove from fire and cool the mixture. Transfer this mixture to a flat surface and chop finely with a knife.

Marination

1. Whisk hung curd in a bowl. Add grated cheese, chopped ginger, coriander leaves, salt, white pepper powder, crushed pepper, black salt, raw mango powder, cornflour and mix well.

2. Add asafoetida mixture to this batter, also add lemon juice, mustard oil and mix well.

3. Put chicken pieces into this mixture, rub well and keep aside to marinate for 2-3 hours.

Cooking

1. Take a skewer and skew the marinated chicken pieces. Keep a tray underneath to collect drippings.

2. Roast in a moderately hot tandoor or over a charcoal grill for 6-7 minutes, until half done.

3. Remove and hang the skewer to let excess moisture drain out completely off (2-3 minutes). Baste with melted butter and roast for another 3-4 minutes.

4. Transfer cooked chicken on to a plate.

5. Serve hot with choice of salad and chutney.

MURG METHI TIKKA

▼

Ingredients

Chicken leg (boneless)	-	850 gm
Ginger garlic paste	-	1 tbsp
Lemon juice	-	2 tbsp
Salt	-	to taste
Fresh methi	-	250 gm
Mustard oil	-	50 ml
Shahi jeera	-	1 tsp
Hung curd	-	300 ml
Garlic paste	-	1 tbsp
Kasoori meethi	-	2 tbsp
Coriander (chopped)	-	10 gm
Green chilli (chopped)	-	3 gm
Ginger (chopped)	-	5 gm
Kashmiri red chilli powder	-	2 tbsp
Garam masala	-	1 tbsp
Chaat masala	-	1 tbsp
Cornflour	-	2 tbsp
Refined oil	-	1 tbsp
Melted butter	-	for basting

TO SERVE: 4

COOKING TIME: 10-12 Minutes

Method

1. Clean, wash and cut each chicken leg into 4 pieces and pat dry with a cloth.
2. In boiling water blanch methi leaves, drain water and make a fine puree in a processor.
3. In a pan heat mustard oil, add shahi jeera. When it crackles, add fresh methi puree. Cook for a while and keep aside to cool.

First Marination

Apply ginger garlic paste, 1 tbsp lemon juice, salt and rub well. Keep aside for 1 hour.

Second Marination

1. In a bowl whisk hung curd. Add garlic paste, kasoori methi powder, chopped coriander, green chilli, ginger, red chilli powder, garam masala, and chaat masala. Add cooked methi puree.
2. Put remaining lemon juice, cornflour, and refined oil and mix well. Adjust seasoning.
3. Remove the excess moisture from the marinated chicken pieces by squeezing the meat with palm.
4. Put chicken pieces into the marinade and rub well. Keep aside for 2-3 hours.

Cooking

1. Take a skewer and skew the marinated chicken pieces one by one. Keep a tray underneath to collect drippings.
2. Roast in a moderately hot tandoor or over a charcoal grill for 6-7 minutes, until half done.
3. Remove and hang the skewer to let excess moisture drain out completely (2-3 minutes). Baste with melted butter and roast for another 3-4 minutes.
4. Transfer chicken on to a plate when cooked.
5. Serve hot with choice of salad and chutney.

CHANDI MURG TIKKA

▼

Ingredients

Chicken breast (boneless)	-	16 nos.
Hung curd	-	300 ml
Grated processed cheese	-	30 gm
Ginger garlic paste	-	1 tbsp
Egg	-	1 no.
Green chilli paste	-	15 gm
Onion (chopped)	-	30 gm
Tomato (chopped)	-	20 gm
Capsicum (chopped)	-	20 gm
Salt	-	to taste
Yellow chilli powder	-	½ tbsp
Shahi jerra	-	½ tbsp
Elaichi powder	-	1 tsp
Crushed white pepper	-	½ tsp
Mixed dry fruit (chopped)	-	50 gm
Lemon juice	-	25 ml
Refined oil	-	80 ml
Chandi ka varq (silver leaf)	-	8 pieces
Melted butter	-	for basting

Method

Clean, wash and cut each chicken breast piece into two. Pat dry and keep aside.

Marination

1. In a bowl whisk hung curd, add grated cheese and ginger garlic paste, egg, green chilli paste, chopped onion, tomato, capsicum, salt, yellow chilli powder, shahi jeera, elaichi powder, crushed while pepper, mix dry fruit, lemon juice, and refined oil and mix well.

2. Put chicken pieces in this mixture and rub well. Keep aside for 2-3 hours.

Cooking

1. Take a skewer and skew the marinated chicken pieces, keep a tray underneath to collect drippings.

2. Roast in a moderately hot tandoor or over a charcoal grill for 4-5 minutes. Until half done.

3. Remove and hang the skewer to let excess moisture drain out completely (2-3 minutes). Baste with melted butter and roast for another 3-4 minutes.

4. Transfer chicken on to a plate, then apply a silver leaf on each breast.

5. Serve hot with choice of salad and chutney.

TO SERVE: 4

COOKING TIME: 8-10 Minutes

GULABI MURG SHASHLIK

▼

Ingredients

Chicken breast (boneless) - 850 gm

Paste

Red rose leaves	-	10 nos.
Boiled onion	-	100 gm
Green chilli	-	10 nos.
Capsicum	-	3 nos.
Onion	-	2 nos.
Tomato	-	3 nos.

Marination

Hung curd	-	300 gm
Cream	-	20 ml
Ginger garlic paste	-	15 gm
Poppy seed paste	-	25 gm
Processed cheese (grated)	-	20 gm
Cornflour	-	15 gm
Roasted gram flour	-	40 gm
Salt	-	to taste
Elaichi powder	-	2 tsp
White pepper powder	-	1 tsp
Rose water	-	10 ml
Refined oil	-	80 ml
Cashewnut paste	-	25 gm
Lemon juice	-	25 ml
Rose petals julienne	-	1 no.
Melted butter	-	for basting

TO SERVE: 4

COOKING TIME: 10-12 Minutes

Method

Clean, wash and cut each chicken piece into half and keep aside.

Paste

1. Put red rose leaves, boiled onions, green chillies in a blender and make a fine paste and keep aside.
2. Cut and deseed capsicum and tomato. Peel and cut onion and cut vegetables into 1-inch square cubes.

Marination

1. In a bowl whisk hung curd, add cream, ginger garlic paste, poppy seed paste, grated cheese, cornflour, and gram flour. Add rose paste, salt, elaichi powder, white pepper powder, rose water, refined oil, cashewnut paste, and lemon juice and mix well.
2. Put chicken pieces and cut vegetables into the above marinade and mix well. Take care to avoid breaking vegetables.
3. Put red rose julienne on top and keep aside for 1-1½ hours.

Cooking

1. Take a skewer and skew the marinated cubes of onion, capsicum, tomatoes, one each on a skewer along with a piece of chicken. Skew the cut vegetables and chicken in the same order.
2. Roast in a moderately hot tandoor or over a charcoal grill for 6-7 minutes.
3. Remove and hang the skewer to let excess moisture drain out completely (2-3 minutes). Baste with melted butter and roast for another 3-4 minutes.
4. Transfer cooked chicken on to a plate.
5. Serve hot with choice of salad and chutney.

▼

Ingredients

Chicken breast (boneless)	-	850 gm
Ginger garlic paste	-	1 tbsp
Green chilli paste	-	1 tsp
Salt	-	to taste
White pepper powder	-	1 tsp
Refined oil	-	10 ml
Processed cheese (grated)	-	200 gm
Egg white	-	1 no.
Cream	-	400 ml
Cashewnut paste	-	50 gm
Ginger garlic paste	-	15 gm
Green chilli paste	-	30 gm
Salt	-	to taste
White pepper powder	-	1 tbsp
Coriander leaves (chopped)	-	30 gm
Green chilly (seedless chopped)	-	15 gm
Refined oil	-	20 ml
Melted butter	-	for basting

TO SERVE: 4

COOKING TIME: 8-10 Minutes

Method

Clean, wash, and cut each chicken breast into 4 pieces. Pat dry with a cloth and keep aside.

First Marination

In a bowl put ginger garlic paste, chilli paste, salt, white pepper powder, and refined oil and mix. Put chicken pieces in this marinade and rub well. Keep for 1 hour.

Second Marination

In a bowl take processed cheese and all the remaining ingredients in the listed order. Mix. Remove the excess moisture from the marinated chicken and put it in the above marinade. Rub well and keep for 2 hours.

Cooking

1. Take a skewer and skew the marinated chicken pieces. Keep a tray underneath to collect drippings.

2. Roast in a moderately hot tandoor or over a charcoal grill for 5-6 minutes.

3. Remove and hang the skewer to let excess moisture drain out completely (2-3 minutes). Baste with melted butter and roast for another 3-4 minutes.

4. Transfer cooked chicken on to a plate.

5. Serve hot with choice of salad and chutney.

▼

▼

Ingredients

Chicken leg (boneless)	-	850 gm
Ginger garlic paste	-	6 tbsp
Boiled onion paste	-	2 tbsp
Roasted besan	-	1 tbsp
Coriander leaves (chopped)	-	2 tbsp
Onion (chopped)	-	2 tbsp
Green chilli (chopped)	-	1 tbsp
Garam masala	-	2 tbsp
Amchoor	-	2 tbsp
Kasoori methi powder	-	1 tbsp
Chaat masala	-	1 tbsp
Kashmiri red chilli powder	-	1 tbsp
Ajwain powder	-	½ tbsp
Vinegar	-	5 tbsp
Salt	-	to taste
Refined oil	-	120 ml
Melted butter	-	for basting

Method

Clean, wash and cut each chicken leg into 4 pieces. Pat dry and keep aside.

Marination

1. In a bowl, put ginger garlic paste and the remaining ingredients in the order listed. Mix well.

2. Put chicken pieces into this marinade. Rub well and keep aside for 2-3 hours.

Cooking

1. Take a skewer and skew the marinated chicken pieces. Keep a tray underneath to collect drippings.

2. Roast in a moderately hot tandoor or over a charcoal grill for 6-7 minutes.

3. Remove and hang the skewer to let excess moisture drain out completely (2-3 minutes). Baste with melted butter and roast for another 3-4 minutes.

4. Transfer cooked chicken on to a plate.

5. Serve hot along with choice of salad and chutney.

TO SERVE: 4

COOKING TIME: 10-12 Minutes

▼

Ingredients

Chicken leg (boneless)   -   850 gm

Paste

Mint leaves	-	100 gm
Coriander leaves	-	250 gm
Boiled spinach	-	50 gm
Green chilli	-	10 nos

First Marination

Ginger garlic paste	-	2 tbsp
Lemon juice	-	20 ml
Salt	-	to taste
Yellow chilli powder	-	½ tsp
Refined oil	-	10 ml

Second Marination

Hung curd	-	100 ml
Garam masala	-	1 tbsp
Mustard oil	-	30 ml
Melted butter	-	for basting

Method

Clean, wash and cut each chicken leg into 4 pieces and pat dry with a cloth.

Paste

Put mint leaves, coriander leaves, spinach, and green chillies in a processor and make a thick paste. Transfer it to a bowl.

First Marination

Apply half ginger garlic paste, 1 tbsp lemon juice, salt, yellow chilli powder, and oil and rub well into the chicken pieces. Keep aside for 1 hour.

Second Marination

In a bowl whisk hung curd, add green paste, ginger garlic paste, salt, garam masala, remaining lemon juice, and mustard oil and mix well.

Cooking

1. Take a skewer and skew the marinated chicken pieces. Keep a tray underneath to collect drippings.

2. Roast in a moderately hot tandoor or over a charcoal grill for 6-7 minutes, until half done.

3. Remove and hang the skewer to let excess moisture drain out completely (2-3 minutes). Baste with melted butter and roast for another 3-4 minutes.

4. Transfer cooked chicken on to a plate.

5. Serve hot with choice of salad and chutney.

TO SERVE: 4

COOKING TIME: 10-12 Minutes

▼

Ingredients

Chicken leg (boneless)	-	850 gm

Paste

Coconut oil	-	30 ml
Mustard seeds	-	½ tsp
Garlic (chopped)	-	I tsp
Ginger (chopped)	-	I tsp
Coriander seeds	-	I tsp
Black cardamom	-	2 nos
Cumin	-	½ tsp
Green cardamom	-	2 nos
Cloves	-	10 nos
Crushed nutmeg	-	½
Poppy seed paste	-	I tbsp
Curry leaves	-	10 nos
Bayleaf	-	2 nos
Whole red chilly	-	5 nos
Brown onion	-	5 gm
Coconut powder	-	10 gm
Chana dal	-	50 gm
Coconut water	-	2 tbsp

First Marination

Ginger garlic paste	-	½ tbsp
Lemon juice	-	10 ml
Salt	-	to taste

Second Marination

Hung curd	-	250 ml
Turmeric	-	a pinch
Tamarind pulp	-	2 tbsp
Coconut oil	-	80 ml
Coconut milk	-	2 tbsp
Salt	-	to taste
Melted butter	-	for basting

TO SERVE: 4

COOKING TIME: 10-12 Minutes

Method

Clean, wash and cut each chicken leg into 4 pieces and pat dry with a cloth.

Paste

Heat coconut oil in a thick bottomed pan. Add all the listed ingredients for the paste and fry until cooked. Cool this mixture and transfer it to a blender to make a fine paste.

First Marination

Apply ginger garlic paste, lemon juice, and salt to the chicken pieces and keep aside for I hour.

Second Marination

1. In a bowl whisk hung curd and the coconut paste, add a pinch of turmeric powder, tamarind pulp, coconut oil and milk. Adjust seasoning and mix well.

2. Remove extra moisture from the chicken pieces by squeezing the chicken lightly between your palms.

3. Put the chicken pieces into the marinade and rub well with the mixture.

Cooking

1. Take a skewer and skew the marinated chicken pieces. Keep a tray underneath to collect drippings.

2. Roast in a moderately hot tandoor or over a charcoal grill for 6-7 minutes, until half done.

3. Remove and hang the skewer to let excess moisture drain out completely (2-3 minutes). Baste with melted butter and roast for another 3-4 minutes.

4. Transfer cooked chicken on to a plate.

5. Serve hot with choice of salad and chutney.

MURG ELAICHI TUKRA

▼

Ingredients

Chicken breast (boneless)	-	850 gm
Hung curd	-	200 gm
Cream	-	100 ml
Salt	-	to taste
Ginger garlic paste	-	1tbsp
Elaichi powder	-	2tbsp
Kashmiri red chilli powder	-	1 tsp
Vinegar	-	15 ml
Cornflour	-	1 tsp
Refined oil	-	80 ml
Melted butter	-	for basting

Method

Clean, wash and cut each chicken breast into half.

Marination

1. In a bowl whisk hung curd, cream, salt ginger garlic paste and add the remaining ingredients in the order listed. Mix well.

2. Put chicken pieces in this mixture and rub well. Keep aside to marinate for 2-3 hours.

Cooking

1. Take a skewer and skew the marinated chicken pieces. Keep a tray underneath to collect drippings.

2. Roast in a moderately hot tandoor or over a charcoal grill for 5-6 minutes.

3. Remove and hang the skewer to let excess moisture drain out completely (2-3 minutes). Baste with melted butter and roast for another 3-4 minutes.

4. Transfer cooked chicken on to a plate.

5. Serve hot with choice of salad and chutney.

TO SERVE: 4

COOKING TIME: 8-10 Minutes

MURG ANARKALI TIKKA

▼

Ingredients

Chicken breast (boneless)	-	850 gm
Pomegranate seeds	-	5 gm
Mint leaves	-	10 gm
Curry leaves	-	10 gm
Coriander leaves	-	10 gm
Green chilli	-	10 gm
Hung curd	-	250 gm
Ginger garlic paste	-	1 tbsp
Onion (chopped)	-	1 tbsp
Ginger (chopped)	-	1 tbsp
Coriander (chopped)	-	1 tbsp
Salt	-	to taste
Kashmiri red chilli powder	-	1 tsp
Garam masala	-	½ tsp
Chaat masala	-	1 tsp
Kasoori methi	-	1 tsp
Lemon juice	-	20 ml
Cornflour	-	1 tbsp
Refined oil	-	80 ml
Melted butter	-	for basting

Method
Clean, wash and cut each chicken breast into half.

Paste
Put pomegranate seeds in a blender with mint, curry leaves, coriander leaves and green chilli and make a fine paste. Transfer this to a bowl.

Marination
Whisk hung curd in a bowl, add paste and the remaining ingredients, and mix well. Put chicken pieces in this mixture and rub well. Keep aside for 2-3 hours.

Cooking
1. Take a skewer and skew the marinated chicken pieces, keep a tray underneath to collect drippings.

2. Roast in a moderately hot tandoor or over a charcoal grill for 6-7 minutes, until half done.

3. Remove and hang the skewer to let excess moisture drain out completely (2-3 minutes). Baste with melted butter and roast for another 2-3 minutes.

4. Transfer cooked chicken on to a plate.

5. Serve hot with choice of salad and chutney.

TO SERVE: 4

COOKING TIME: 8-10 Minutes

RESHMI MURG TIKKA

▼

Ingredients

Chicken leg (boneless)	-	850 gm
Refined oil	-	100 ml
Onion (chopped)	-	20 gm
Garlic (chopped)	-	10 gm
Gram flour	-	100 gm

First Marination

Ginger garlic paste	-	1 tbsp
Salt	-	to taste
White pepper powder	-	2 tbsp
White vinegar	-	20 ml

Second Marination

Cashewnut paste	-	200 gm
Cream	-	100 ml
Ginger garlic paste	-	1 tbsp
Salt	-	to taste
White pepper powder	-	1 tbsp
Melted butter	-	for basting

Method

1. Clean and wash the chicken legs cut into large cube size.

2. Heat oil in a pan add chopped onion and garlic and saute for a while, add gram flour and slightly saute so that it doesn't change its colour. Leave to cool.

First Marination

Apply the ginger garlic paste, salt, white pepper powder, and vinegar to the chicken pieces and keep it for 1 hour.

Second Marination

1. In a bowl, take cashewnut paste, roasted gram flour mixture, cream, garlic ginger paste, salt and white pepper powder and mix.

2. Put the marinated chicken in this mixture and rub well and keep aside for 3 hours.

Cooking

1. Take a skewer and skew the marinated chicken pieces. Keep a tray underneath to collect drippings.

2. Roast in a moderately hot tandoor or over a charcoal grill for 6-7 minutes, until half done.

3. Remove and hang the skewer to let excess moisture drain out completely (2-3 minutes). Baste with melted butter and roast for another 3-4 minutes.

4. Transfer cooked chicken on to a plate.

5. Serve hot with choice of salad and chutney.

TO SERVE: 4

COOKING TIME: 10-12 Minutes

KASOORI MURG TIKKA

▼

Ingredients

Chicken leg (boneless)	-	850 gm
Refined oil	-	100 ml
Onion (chopped)	-	20 gm
Garlic (chopped)	-	10 gm
Gram flour	-	100 gm

First Marination

Ginger garlic paste	-	1 tbsp
Salt	-	to taste
White pepper powder	-	2 tbsp
White vinegar	-	20 ml

Second Marination

Cashewnut paste	-	200 gm
Cream	-	100 ml
Ginger garlic paste	-	1 tbsp
Salt	-	to taste
White pepper powder	-	1 tbsp
Kasoori methi	-	2 tbsp
Melted butter	-	for basting

Method

1. Clean and wash the chicken legs and cut into large cubes.

2. Heat oil in a pan. Add chopped onion, garlic and saute for a while. Add gram flour and slightly saute so that it doesn't change its colour. Leave to cool.

First Marination

Apply the ginger garlic paste, salt, white pepper powder, and vinegar to chicken pieces and keep it for 1 hour.

Second Marination

1. In a bowl take cashewnut paste, roasted gram flour mixture, cream, ginger garlic paste, salt, white pepper powder, and kasoori methi and mix.

2. Put marinated chicken in this mixture, rub well and keep aside for 3 hours.

Cooking

1. Take a skewer and skew the marinated chicken pieces, keep a tray underneath to collect drippings.

2. Roast in a moderately hot tandoor or over a charcoal grill for 6-7 minutes, until half done.

3. Remove and hang the skewer to let excess moisture drain out completely (2-3 minutes). Baste with melted butter and roast for another 3-4 minutes.

4. Transfer cooked chicken on to a plate.

5. Serve hot with choice of salad and chutney.

TO SERVE: 4

COOKING TIME: 10-12 Minutes

MURG MALAI KEBAB

▼

Ingredients
Chicken breast (boneless) - 850 gm

First Marination
Ginger garlic paste	-	1 tbsp
Lemon juice	-	10 ml
Salt	-	to taste

Second Marination
Processed cheese	-	50 gm
Egg white	-	1 nos
Ginger garlic paste	-	2 tbsp
Cashewnut paste	-	3 tbsp
Green chilli paste	-	1 tbsp
Cream	-	200 ml
Cornflour	-	2 tsp
Elaichi javitri powder	-	1 tsp
White pepper powder	-	½ tbsp
Shahi jeera	-	1 tbsp
Salt	-	to taste
Refined oil	-	80 ml
Melted butter	-	for basting

Method
Clean, wash and cut each chicken breast into half and pat dry with a cloth.

First Marination
Apply ginger garlic paste, lemon juice, and salt to the chicken and keep aside for 1 hour.

Second Marination
1. In a deep tray put grated cheese, and mix gradually with your palm. Pow cream and further mix so that it becomes a smooth paste. Add remaining ingredients as listed and mix well.

2. Remove the extra moisture from the chicken pieces. Mix the chicken pieces with the marinade and rub well. Keep aside for 2 hours.

Cooking
1. Take a skewer and skew the marinated chicken pieces. Keep a tray underneath to collect drippings.

2. Roast in a moderately hot tandoor or over a charcoal grill for 5-7 minutes, until half done.

3. Remove and hang the skewer to let excess moisture drain out completely (2-3 minutes). Baste with melted butter and roast for another 2-3 minutes.

4. Transfer cooked chicken on to a plate.

5. Serve hot with choice of salad and chutney.

TO SERVE: 4

COOKING TIME: 10-12 Minutes

▼

Ingredients

Chicken leg (boneless)	-	850 gm
Betel leaves	-	150 gm
Hung curd	-	180 gm
Cashewnut paste	-	2 tbsp
Ginger garlic paste	-	1 tbsp
Kewra water	-	1 tsp
Rose water	-	1 tsp
Garam masala	-	1 tbsp
Kashmiri red chilli powder	-	2 tsp
Lemon juice	-	2 tbsp
Refined oil	-	80 ml
Salt	-	to taste
Melted butter	-	for basting

Method

1. Clean, wash and cut each chicken leg into 4 pieces and pat dry with a cloth.

2. Wash betel leaves, put them in a processor, add a few drops of water and make a fine paste. Transfer to a bowl.

Marination

1. In a bowl whisk hung curd with the betel leaf paste, cashew nut paste, ginger garlic paste, kewra water, rose water and the remaining ingredients. Mix well.

2. Put the chicken pieces into this marinade and rub well. Keep aside for 2-3 hours. (The marinade could be kept overnight in case a strong flavour of betel leaves is desired.)

Cooking

1. Take a skewer and skew the marinated chicken pieces. Keep a tray underneath to collect drippings.

2. Roast in a moderately hot tandoor or over a charcoal grill for 6-7 minutes, until half done.

3. Remove and hang the skewer to let excess moisture drain out completely (2-3 minutes). Baste with melted butter and roast for another 3-4 minutes.

4. Transfer cooked chicken on to a plate.

5. Serve hot with choice of salad and chutney.

TO SERVE: 4

COOKING TIME: 10-12 Minutes

▼

Ingredients

Chicken leg (boneless)	-	850 gm
Salt	-	to taste
Red chilli paste	-	1 tbsp
Lemon juice	-	10 ml
Ginger garlic paste	-	1 tbsp
Soya sauce	-	5 tbsp
Worcesterchire sauce	-	1 tbsp
Tomato ketchup	-	4 tbsp
Vinegar	-	10 ml
Sugar	-	25 gm
Cornflour	-	50 gm
Melted butter	-	for basting

Method

Clean and cut each chicken leg into 4 pieces.

First Marination

Apply salt, red chilli paste, lemon juice and ginger garlic paste to chicken and keep it for 1 hour.

Second Marination

1. In a bowl, take soya sauce and mix all the ingredients in the order listed.

2. Marinate chicken in the prepared mixture for 2 hours.

Cooking

1. Take a skewer and skew the marinated chicken pieces. Keep a tray underneath to collect drippings.

2. Roast in a moderately hot tandoor or over a charcoal grill for 6-7 minutes.

3. Hang the skewer to let excess moisture drain out completely (2-3 minutes). Baste with melted butter and roast for another 2-3 minutes.

4. Transfer cooked chicken on to a plate.

5. Serve hot with choice of salad and chutney.

TO SERVE: 4

COOKING TIME: 10-12 Minutes

TANDOORI MURG PESHAWARI

▼

Ingredients

Chicken (whole)	-	4 nos.
Ginger garlic paste	-	1 tbsp
Red chilli paste	-	1 tbsp
Salt	-	to taste
Lemon juice	-	25 ml
Hung curd	-	400 ml
Ginger garlic paste	-	1 tbsp
Garam masala	-	2 tbsp
Kasoori methi powder	-	1 tbsp
Refined oil	-	80 ml
Chaat masala	-	2 tbsp
Lemon juice	-	60 ml
Melted butter	-	for basting

Method

Clean, wash and make three incisions with a sharp knife on breast and leg.

First Marination

Apply ginger garlic paste, red chilli paste, salt and lemon juice. Rub mixture all around the chicken and keep aside for 1 hour.

Second Marination

1. In a bowl, whisk hung curd, add ginger garlic paste, garam masala, oil and kasoori methi powder. Mix well.

2. Put marinated chicken into this marinade, and rub throughly all around. Keep aside for 2-3 hours.

Cooking

1. Take a skewer and skew the marinated chicken from tail to head leaving a gap of 2-3 inches between the buds.

2. Roast in a moderately hot tandoor or over a charcoal grill for 12-15 minutes.

3. Remove and hang the skewer so as to let the excess moisture drain out completely (2-3 minutes).

4. Baste with melted butter and roast again for 5-7 minutes.

5. Cut chicken into 4 pieces. Sprinkle chaat masala and lemon juice.

6. Serve hot with choice of salad and chutney.

TO SERVE: 4

COOKING TIME: 15-20 Minutes

▼

TANDOORI MURG FRONTIER

▼

Ingredients

Chicken (skinless)	-	2 nos. (600-650 gm each)
Salt	-	to taste
Red chilli powder	-	1 tsp
Lemon juice	-	30 ml
Hung curd	-	300 gm
Red chilli powder	-	2 tsp
Ginger paste	-	30 gm
Garlic paste	-	30 gm
Tandoori masala	-	a pinch
Melted butter	-	for basting

Method

Clean, wash and cut each chicken into 2 parts from the back bone. Make deep incisions, at least 3 on each breast and leg. Sprinkle salt, red chilly powder, lemon juice and rub over the chicken. Keep aside.

Marination

Whisk hung curd in a bowl, add red chilli powder, ginger paste, and garlic paste and mix well. Dip chicken in the mixture and rub well. Keep to marinate for 3-4 hours.

Cooking

1. Take a skewer and skew marinated chicken from tail to head, leaving a gap of at least 2-3 inches between the chicken pieces.

2. Roast in a moderately hot tandoor or over a charcoal grill for 10-15 minutes until half done.

3. Hang the skewer to let the excess moisture drain out completely for 4-5 minutes. Baste with melted butter and roast further for 4-5 minutes until done.

4. Remove from skewer, cut each chicken into 4 pieces.

5. Sprinkle tandoori masala. Serve hot with choice of salad and chutney.

TO SERVE: 4

COOKING TIME: 15-20 Minutes

▼

Ingredients

Chicken drumsticks	-	16 nos.
Ginger garlic paste	-	1 tbsp
Lemon juice	-	1 tbsp
Salt	-	to taste
Hung curd	-	350 gm
Cream	-	50 ml
Processed (grated) cheese	-	40 gm
Ginger garlic paste	-	2 tbsp
Sesame seed paste	-	100 gm
Kashmiri red chilli powder	-	2 tbsp
Garam masala	-	1 tbsp
White vinegar	-	2 tbsp
Melted butter	-	for basting

Method

Clean, wash and make incisions on chicken legs with the help of a sharp knife. At least three on each side.

First Marination

Apply ginger garlic paste, lemon juice, and salt to the chicken legs and keep aside for 1 hour.

Second Marination

1. In a bowl, whisk hung curd and add the remaining ingredients in the order listed and mix well.

2. After squeezing excess moisture put chicken pieces into this marinade. Rub well and keep aside for 2-3 hours.

Cooking

1. Take a skewer and skew chicken legs horizontally, leaving a gap of at least an inch between the legs.

2. Roast in a moderately hot tandoor or over a charcoal grill for approx. 10-12 minutes.

3. Remove and hang skewer so that the excess moisture drain out completely (2-3 minutes). Baste with melted butter and further roast for 3-4 minutes.

4. Serve hot with choice of salad and chutney.

TO SERVE: 4

COOKING TIME: 12-15 Minutes

Ingredients

Chicken leg	-	8 nos. (850 gm)
Hung curd	-	150 gm
Cashewnut paste	-	5 tbsp
Processed cheese (granted)	-	20 gm
Cream	-	125 ml
Grated khoya	-	50 gm
Brown onion paste	-	2 tbsp
Egg yolk	-	2 nos.
Elaichi javitri powder	-	1 tsp
Coriander (chopped)	-	2 tbsp
Ginger (chopped)	-	1 tsp
Green chilli (chopped)	-	1 tsp
Shahi jeera	-	½ tsp
Ginger garlic paste	-	1 tbsp
White pepper powder	-	2 tsp
Lemon juice	-	1 tsp
Malt vinegar	-	1 tsp
Cornflour	-	1 tbsp
Salt	-	to taste
Ghee	-	10 ml
Cloves	-	6 nos.
Melted butter	-	for basting

TO SERVE: 4

COOKING TIME: 10-12 Minutes

Method

Clean, wash and flatten each chicken leg with a hammer and pat dry with a cloth and keep aside.

Marination

1. In a bowl whisk hung curd and add the remaining ingredients in the order listed and mix.

2. Put chicken pieces and rub well with this mixture. Keep aside for 2-3 hours.

3. Take 4-5 pieces of burning charcoal in a small bowl and keep it along the marinated chicken. Put cloves and pour ghee on top and immediately cover the patila with a lid for 3-5 minutes to give a smoking flavour.

Cooking

1. Take a skewer and skew the marinated chicken pieces. Keep a tray underneath to collect drippings.

2. Roast in a moderately hot tandoor or over a charcoal grill for 6-7 minutes, until half done.

3. Remove and hang the skewer to let excess moisture drain out completely (2-3 minutes). Baste with melted butter and roast for another 3-4 minutes.

4. Transfer cooked chicken on to a plate.

5. Serve hot with choice of salad and chutney.

HARYALI CHOOZA KEBAB

▼

Ingredients

Chicken leg	-	16 nos.
Mint leaves	-	100 gm
Fresh coriander leaves	-	250 gm
Boiled spinach	-	50 gm
Green chilli	-	10 nos.
Black salt	-	to taste
Ginger garlic paste	-	2 tbsp
Lemon juice	-	20 ml
Salt	-	to taste
Hung curd	-	100 ml
Garam masala	-	½ tbsp
Mustard oil	-	30 ml
Melted butter	-	for basting

TO SERVE: 4

COOKING TIME: 12-15 Minutes

Method

1. Clean, wash and make incisions on chicken legs with the help of a sharp knife, at least three on each side. Keep aside.

2. In a processor/blender put mint leaves, coriander, spinach, green chilli, and black salt and make a fine paste. Transfer it to a bowl.

First Marination

Apply 1 tbsp ginger garlic paste half lemon juice and salt to the chicken legs and leave aside for 1 hour.

Second Marination

1. In a bowl whisk hung curd and add green paste, remaining ginger garlic paste, salt, garam masala, lemon juice, and mustard oil and mix well.

2. Remove the excess moisture from the chicken pieces and mix well with these ingredients. Keep aside for 2 hours.

Cooking

1. Take a skewer and skew the marinated chicken pieces. Keep a tray underneath to collect drippings.

2. Roast in a moderately hot tandoor or over a charcoal grill for 6-7 minutes.

3. Remove and hang the skewer to let excess moisture drain out completely (2-3 minutes). Baste with melted butter and roast for another 3-4 minutes.

4. Transfer cooked chicken on to a plate.

5. Serve hot with choice of salad and chutney.

MURG SEEKH NURANI

▼

Ingredients

Whole chicken breast	-	850 gm
Garlic paste	-	200 gm
Hung curd	-	350 gm
Cream	-	150 ml
Garlic (chopped)	-	100 gm
Salt	-	to taste
Kashmiri red chilli powder	-	4 tbsp
Turmeric powder	-	1 tbsp
Garam masala	-	1 tbsp
Chaat masala	-	1 tbsp
Lemon juice	-	100 ml
Roasted gram flour	-	4 tbsp
Refined oil	-	100 ml
Melted butter	-	30 ml

Method

Clean and remove the winglet bone from the chicken breast. Apply garlic paste, rub well and keep aside.

Marination

1. In a bowl whisk hung curd, add the remaining ingredients in the order listed and mix thoroughly.

2. Remove extra moisture from the marinated chicken breast and add it to the above marinade. Keep refrigerated for 2-3 hours.

Cooking

1. Take a skewer and skew marinated chicken breasts carefully, flat an inch apart. Do not fold.

2. Roast in a moderate hot tandoor or over a charcoal grill for 8-10 minutes.

3. Remove and hang to let excess moisture drain out completely (2-3 minutes).

4. Baste with melted butter and roast further for 3-4 minutes.

5. Serve hot along with choice of salad and chutney.

TO SERVE: 4

COOKING TIME: 10-12 Minutes

▼

Ingredients

Chicken thigh	-	16 nos.
Ginger garlic paste	-	1 tbsp
Red chilli paste	-	1 tbsp
Salt	-	to taste
White pepper powder	-	1 tbsp
Vinegar	-	10 ml
Refined oil	-	90 ml
Hung curd	-	350 ml
Cream	-	100 ml
Grated cheese	-	50 gm
Ginger garlic paste	-	1 tbsp
Red chilli paste	-	4 tbsp
Salt	-	to taste
Garam masala powder	-	1 tbsp
Coriander powder	-	1 tbsp
Crushed peppercorn	-	1 tbsp
Gulab jal	-	2 drops
Refined oil	-	80 ml
Melted butter	-	30 ml

Method

Clean and remove thigh bone from one side and cut the flesh into two equal parts. Pat dry and keep aside.

First Marination

In a bowl put ginger garlic paste, red chilly paste, salt, white pepper powder, vinegar, oil and and mix well. Add chicken pieces and rub well. Keep the chicken for 1 hour.

Second Marination

1. Whisk hung curd in a bowl, and add the remaining ingredients in the order listed. Mix well.

2. Put marinated chicken pieces in this mixture, rub well and leave for 2-3 hours.

Cooking

1. Take a skewer and skew the marinated chicken pieces. Keep a tray underneath to collect drippings.

2. Roast in a moderately hot tandoor or over a charcoal grill for 10-12 minutes.

3. Remove and hang the skewer to let excess moisture drain out completely (2-3 minutes). Baste with melted butter and roast for another 3-4 minutes.

4. Transfer cooked chicken on to a plate.

5. Serve hot with choice of salad and chutney.

TO SERVE: 4

COOKING TIME: 12-15 Minutes

▼

Ingredients

Chicken (medium size)	-	2 nos.
Capsicum	-	75 gm
Tomato	-	75 gm
Onion	-	75 gm
Ginger garlic paste	-	1 tbsp
Salt	-	to taste
White pepper powder	-	1 tbsp
Vinegar	-	10 ml
Refined oil	-	10 ml
Hung curd	-	250 ml
Cashewnut paste	-	100 gm
Green chilli (chopped)	-	10 gm
Coriander leaves (chopped)	-	20 gm
Elaichi javitri powder	-	½ tsp
Crushed peppercorn	-	1 tsp
Melted butter	-	for basting

Method

1. Clean and cut each chicken into 8 pieces. Pat dry and keep aside.

2. Cut capsicum into 4 and deseed. Cut tomatoes into 4 and deseed. Peel and cut onions into 4. Cut these vegetables into large cubes.

First Marination

In a bowl put ginger garlic paste, salt, white pepper powder, vinegar, oil and mix. Put chicken pieces, rub well and keep it for 1 hour.

Second Marination

1. In a bowl take hung curd and add all the remaining ingredients in the order listed.

2. Squeeze excess moisture from the marinated chicken and add it to the above marinade. Rub well and keep aside for 1-2 hours.

Cooking

1. Take a skewer and skew the marinated chicken pieces and the vegetables along the skewer alternately. Keep a tray underneath to collect drippings.

2. Roast in a moderately hot tandoor or over a charcoal grill for 6-7 minutes.

3. Remove and hang the skewer to let excess moisture drain out completely (2-3 minutes). Baste with melted butter and roast for another 5-6 minutes.

4. Transfer cooked chicken on to a plate.

5. Serve hot with choice of salad and chutney.

TO SERVE: 4

COOKING TIME: 12-15 Minutes

▼

Ingredients

Chicken leg   -   16 nos.

First Marination

Ginger garlic paste	-	I tbsp
Red chilli paste	-	I tbsp
Salt	-	to taste
Refined oil	-	10 ml
Vinegar	-	10 ml

Second Marination

Hung curd	-	250 ml
Ginger garlic paste	-	I tbsp
Red chilli paste	-	2 tbsp
Salt	-	to taste
White pepper powder	-	I tbsp
Garam masala	-	I tbsp
Cinnamon powder	-	I tbsp
Elaichi dana (crushed)	-	I tsp
Crushed pepper corn	-	2 tsp
Lemon juice	-	20 ml
Refined oil	-	40 ml
Melted butter	-	for basting

Method

Clean and wash chicken leg and make incisions, at least 3 on each side. Pat dry and keep aside.

First Marination

In a bowl put ginger garlic paste, red chilli paste, salt, oil, vinegar and mix. Add chicken pieces, rub well and keep aside for I hour.

Second Marination

In a bowl take hung curd and all the remaining ingredients in the order listed. Mix well. Remove excess water from the marinated chicken pieces and add it to the marination and leave for 2 hours.

Cooking

1. Take a skewer and skew the marinated chicken pieces. Keep a tray underneath to collect drippings.

2. Roast in a moderately hot tandoor or over a charcoal grill for 8-10 minutes.

3. Remove and hang the skewer to let excess moisture drain out completely (2-3 minutes). Baste with melted butter and roast for another 2-3 minutes.

4. Transfer cooked chicken on to a plate.

5. Serve hot with choice of salad and chutney.

TO SERVE: 4

COOKING TIME: 12-15 Minutes

LAZEEZ BHARWAN MURG SEENA

▼

Ingredients

Chicken breast (with bone) - 8 nos.

Stuffing

Same as for potli kebab + saffron + kewra water	-	10 ml
Clove powder	-	1 tsp
Processed Cheese (grated)	-	50/75 gm
Hung curd	-	300 ml
Cream	-	150 ml
Cashew nut paste	-	60 gm
Egg yolk	-	1 no.
Chopped garlic	-	30 gm
Salt	-	to taste
Clove powder	-	1 tsp
Crushed peppercorn	-	1 tsp
Elaichi powder	-	1 tsp
Raw mango powder	-	1 tsp
Cornflour	-	2 tbsp
Lemon juice	-	25 ml
Malt vinegar	-	15 ml
Refined oil	-	80 ml
Melted butter	-	for basting

TO SERVE: 4

COOKING TIME: 12-15 Minutes

Method

Clean chicken breast and with a sharp knife, slit it from the wings. Make a hole with the help of a finger at least 1 inch deep.

Stuffing

1. As for potli kebab with an addition of kesar and kewra water, clove powder, grated cheese. Cool and keep aside.

2. Stuff each breast with this mixture and skew each with a toothpick so that the stuffing does not come out.

Marination

In a bowl, whisk hung curd and add the remaining ingredients in the order listed. Mix thoroughly and put stuffed chicken breast into this mixture. Apply all around and keep it for 2 hours.

Cooking

1. Take a skewer and skew marinated chicken breast carefully, an inch apart from the edge of shoulder bone.

2. Roast in a moderate hot tandoor for about 8-10 minutes.

3. Remove and hang skewer to let excess moisture drain out completely (2-3 minutes).

4. Baste with melted butter and roast for another 4-5 minutes.

5. Transfer cooked chicken breast on to a plate.

6. Serve hot along with choice of salad and chutney.

TANDOORI BATER

▼

Ingredients

Quail (bater)	-	8 nos.
Salt	-	to taste
Red chilli paste	-	1 tbsp
Ginger garlic paste	-	2 tbsp
Lemon juice	-	15 ml
Hung curd	-	300 ml
Kasoori methi powder	-	1 tsp
Garam masala	-	1 tsp
Refined oil	-	30 ml
Melted butter	-	for basting

Method

Cut, clean, wash the bater and keep aside.

First Marination

In a bowl take salt, half of red chilli paste, ginger garlic paste, lemon juice and mix well. Apply this marinade to the bater. Rub well and keep aside for 1-2 hours.

Second Marination

1. In a bowl whisk hung curd, add remaining ginger garlic paste, remaining red chilli paste, salt, kasoori methi powder, garam masala and refined oil. Mix well.

2. Remove excess moisture from the bater by slightly squeezing it with your palm and dip in the above marinade. Leave for 2 hours.

Cooking

1. Take a skewer and skew marinated bater from tail to head one by one. Apply remaining marinade on top.

2. Roast in a moderately hot tandoor or over a charcoal grill for 6-8 minutes.

3. Remove and hang to let excess moisture drain out completely (2-3 minutes).

4. Baste with melted butter and further roast for 3-4 minutes.

5. Transfer on to a plate when cooked.

6. Serve hot along with choice of salad and chutney.

TO SERVE: 4

COOKING TIME: 10-12 Minutes

PANKHARI KEBAB

▼

Ingredients

Murg pankhari (chicken
wings and shoulder)   -   24 nos.

First Marination

Ginger garlic paste	-	I tbsp
Salt	-	to taste
White pepper powder	-	I tsp

Second Marination

Processed cheese (grated)	-	150 gm
Egg white	-	I nos.
Cream	-	300 ml
Ginger garlic paste	-	I tbsp
Salt	-	to taste
White pepper powder	-	½ tbsp
Dalchini powder	-	I tsp
Green chilli (chopped)	-	15 gm
Melted butter	-	30 ml

TO SERVE: 4

COOKING TIME: 8-10 Minutes

Method

Cut and clean chicken wings and shoulder. Wash, pat
dry and keep aside.

First Marination

In a bowl take ginger garlic paste, salt, white pepper
powder. Dip chicken pankhari, rub well and leave for
1 hour.

Second Marination

1. In a tray put cheese, add egg white and rub it
   with your palm in one direction. Add cream
   gradually so that it gets blended. Add ginger garlic
   paste, salt and all the remaining ingredients in the
   order listed. Mix well.

2. Dip murg pankhari in the above marinade and
   keep aside for 1-2 hours.

Cooking

1. Take a skewer and skew marinated pankhari pieces
   one by one, leaving a gap of an inch between the
   wings.

2. Roast in a moderate tandoor or over a charcoal
   grill for 4-6 minutes.

3. Remove and hang so that excess moisture driains
   out completely off (2-3 minutes).

4. Baste with melted butter and again roast for
   2-3 minutes.

5. Serve hot with choice of salad and chutney.

▼

Ingredients

Chicken mince	-	800 gm
Processed cheese (grated)	-	80 gm
Cream	-	80 ml
Ginger garlic paste	-	15 gm
Green chilli (chopped)	-	5 gm
Coriander (chopped)	-	15 gm
Salt	-	to taste
Elaichi javitri powder	-	a pinch
White pepper powder	-	½ tbsp
Melted butter	-	for basting

Method

1. Take chicken mince in a bowl.

2. Add grated cheese, cream, ginger garlic paste and mix thoroughly with your palm. Add chopped green chilli, coriander, salt, elaichi javitri powder, and white pepper powder and mix well. Keep aside for 30 minutes.

Cooking

1. Divide marinated mince into 16 equal portions and make balls.

2. Take a skewer using a wet palm, spread this mixture along the length of the skewer in a cylindrical shape and an inch apart to make each kebab 4 inches long.

3. Roast in a moderately hot tandoor or over a charcoal grill for 4-5 minutes.

4. Remove and hang so that the excess moisture drains out completely (2-3 minutes). Baste with melted butter and further cook until light golden (2-3 minutes).

5. Transfer on to a plate and serve hot with choice of salad and chutney.

TO SERVE: 4

COOKING TIME: 6-8 Minutes

PHULJHARI SEEKH KEBAB

▼

Ingredients

Chicken mince	-	650 gm
Grated processed cheese	-	60 gm
Ginger garlic paste	-	2 tbsp
Green chilli (chopped)	-	2 tbsp
Coriander (chopped)	-	4 tbsp
Ginger (chopped)	-	2 tbsp
Elaichi javitri powder	-	1 tbsp
White pepper powder	-	1 tbsp
Kasoori methi powder	-	1 tbsp
Egg yolk	-	2 nos
Kandhari anar seeds	-	4 tbsp
Refined oil	-	4 tbsp
Salt	-	to taste
Onion (chopped very fine)	-	12 tbsp
Melted butter	-	for basting

Method

1. In a bowl take chicken mince and add grated cheese, ginger garlic paste and rub well.

2. Add the remaining ingredients except anar seeds and chopped onions in the order listed. Rub well with open palm. Correct seasoning.

3. Now add anar seeds and mix. Divide this mince into 16 equal portions and make balls.

Cooking

1. Take a skewer, using a wet palm, spread each ball along the length of skewer in a cylindrical shape, 2 inches apart, making each kebab 4 inches long.

2. Apply finely chopped onion on top of the seekh with a light hand and roast in a tandoor or over a charcoal grill for 4-5 minutes.

3. Baste it with melted butter and further roast it in a tandoor for 2-3 minutes.

4. Serve hot along with choice of salad and chutney.

TO SERVE: 4

COOKING TIME: 6-8 Minutes

▼

MISSI MASALA SEEKH

▼

Ingredients

Chicken mince	-	600 gm
Boiled egg yolk	-	4 nos.
Mint (chopped)	-	2 tsp
Coriander (chopped)	-	4 tbsp
Green chilly (chopped)	-	2 tsp
Ginger (chopped)	-	1 tbsp
Roasted ajwain	-	2 tsp
Crushed anardana	-	3 tbsp
Shahi jeera	-	2 tsp
Amchoor powder	-	2 tsp
Red chilli powder	-	2 tsp
Garam masala	-	2 tsp
Roasted besan	-	2 tbsp
Brown onion paste	-	4 tbsp
Lemon juice	-	2 tbsp
Mustard oil	-	60 ml
Salt	-	to taste

For Coating

Egg yolk	-	6 nos.
Mint (chopped)	-	2 tbsp
Coriander (chopped)	-	2 tbsp
Melted butter	-	for basting

TO SERVE: 4

COOKING TIME: 8-10 Minutes

Method

1. In a bowl take chicken mince, grate the boiled egg yolk into it, add chopped vegetable, roasted ajwain and mix.

2. Add crushed anardana, shahi jeera, and rub well with your palm. Add the remaining ingredients and adjust seasoning.

3. Divide this mixture into 16 equal portions and make balls.

4. In a separate bowl, whisk egg yolk, add chopped mint, and coriander and mix.

Cooking

1. Take a skewer and using wet hands apply each ball along the skewer in a cylindrical shape, 2 inches apart making each kebab 4 inches long.

2. Coat each seekh with egg yolk mixture all over and roast in tandoor or over a charcoal grill for 5-6 minutes. Baste with melted butter and further roast for 3-4 minutes.

3. Serve hot along with choice of salad and chutney.

SANGAM SEEKH KEBAB

▼

Ingredients

Chicken mince	-	350 gm
Mutton mince	-	350 gm
Grated processed cheese	-	20 gm
Ginger garlic paste	-	1 tbsp
Ginger (chopped)	-	1 tbsp
Garlic (chopped)	-	1 tbsp
Fried curry leaves	-	a few
Kashmiri red chilli powder	-	1 tbsp
Shehenshahi masala	-	1 tsp
Egg yolk	-	1 no.
Lemon juice	-	1 tsp
Turmeric powder	-	½ tsp
Saffron	-	a pinch
Kewra water	-	1 tbsp
Salt	-	to taste
Spring onion (green) (chopped)	-	1 tbsp
Coriander (chopped)	-	1 tbsp
Melted butter	-	for basting

Method

1. In a bowl put chicken and mutton mince and add grated cheese, ginger garlic paste, chopped ginger and garlic, fried curry leaves, kashmiri red chilli powder, shehenshahi masala, egg yolk, lemon juice. Mix well.

2. Divide this mince into 2 equal portions.

3. Keep one part aside. To the other half add the remaining ingredients and mix well.

4. Adjust seasoning in both the mixtures and divide both the mixtures into 16 equal portions and make balls.

Cooking

1. Take a skewer, and using wet hands adjust each mince ball along the skewer lengthwise in a cylindrical shape, 2 inches apart, making each seekh 4 inches long.

2. Roast it in a tandoor at a moderate temperature for 2-3 minutes.

3. Apply the second half of the mixture over the same seekh carefully with a wet hand. Further roast for 4-6 minutes.

4. Baste with melted butter and further roast for 2-3 minutes.

5. Serve hot with choice of salad and chutney.

TO SERVE: 4

COOKING TIME: 8-10 Minutes

DHUANDHAR RESHMI KEBAB

▼

Ingredients

Chicken mince	-	800 gm
Grated processed cheese	-	50 gm
Cream	-	100 ml
Melon seed paste	-	30 gm
Ginger garlic paste	-	15 gm
Salt	-	to taste
Garam masala	-	½ tbsp
White pepper powder	-	½ tbsp
Coriander (chopped)	-	30 gm
Green chilly (chopped)	-	15 gm
Ghee	-	10 ml
Cloves	-	6 nos
Melted butter	-	30 ml

Method

1. In a bowl take chicken mince and add grated cheese, cream, melon seed paste and ginger garlic paste. Mix well.

2. Add salt, garam masala, white pepper powder, chopped coriander and green chilli and mix. Transfer this to a large patila and keep aside.

3. Take 4-5 pieces of burning charcoal in a katori and keep it along the chicken mince. Put cloves and pour ghee on top and immediately cover the patila with a lid for 3-5 minutes to give it a smoking flavour.

4. Divide this mixture into 16 equal parts and make balls.

Cooking

1. Take a skewer and spread this mixture using a wet palm. Press each kebab along the length of the skewer in a cylindrical shape, one inch apart, making each kebab 4 inches long.

2. Roast in a moderately hot tandoor or over a charcoal grill for 5-6 minutes. Baste with melted butter and further roast for 2-3 minutes.

3. Serve hot along with choice of salad and chutney.

TO SERVE: 4

COOKING TIME: 6-8 Minutes

MURG KALONJI SEEKH

▼

Ingredients

Chicken mince	-	650 gm
Cashewnut paste	-	2 tbsp
Ginger garlic paste	-	2 tbsp
Grated processed cheese	-	40 gm
Onion (chopped)	-	2 tbsp
Coriander (chopped)	-	2 tbsp
Green chilli (chopped)	-	1 tbsp
Ginger (chopped)	-	1 tbsp
Kebab chini powder	-	a pinch
Amchoor	-	2 tsp
Kashmiri red chilli powder	-	2 tsp
White pepper powder	-	1 tsp
Egg yolk	-	2 nos
Salt	-	to taste

For Applying on Seekh

Kalonji seeds	-	2 tbsp
Mustard seeds	-	1 tbsp
Sesame seeds	-	1 tbsp
Coriander (chopped)	-	1 tbsp
Ginger julienne	-	1 tbsp
Melted butter	-	for basting

TO SERVE: 4

COOKING TIME: 6-8 Minutes

Method

1. In a bowl take chicken mince, cashewnut paste, ginger garlic paste, and grated cheese. Mix well with your palm.

2. Put chopped vegetables, a pinch of kebab chini masala, amchoor, red chilli powder, and egg yolk and rub well. Correct seasoning and keep aside.

3. Heat a non-stick pan, broil the mustard seeds, kalonji and sesame seeds for a few seconds. Add this to the chicken mince along with julienne of ginger and chopped coriander. Keep aside.

4. Divide this mixture into 16 equal parts and make balls.

Cooking

1. Take a skewer and spread this mixture using a wet palm along the length of the skewer in a cylindrical shape one inch apart and make each kebab 4 inches long.

2. Roast in a moderately hot tandoor or over a charcoal grill for 4-5 minutes. Baste with melted butter and further roast for 2-3 minutes.

3. Serve hot along with choice of salad and chutney.

MURG METHI SEEKH KEBAB

▼

Ingredients

Chicken mince	-	500 gm
Mustard oil	-	30 gm
Cumin seeds	-	1 tsp
Garlic (chopped)	-	30 gm
Methi leaves (chopped)	-	200 gm
Garlic paste	-	15 gm
Egg yolk	-	1 nos.
Grated processed cheese	-	50 gm
Onion (chopped)	-	50 gm
Green chilli (chopped)	-	10 gm
Salt	-	to taste
Red chilli powder	-	1 tbsp
Kebab chini powder	-	1 tbsp
Garam masala	-	1 tbsp
Kastoori methi powder	-	1 tbsp
Melted butter	-	30 ml

Method

1. In a bowl take chicken mince and keep aside.

2. Heat mustard oil in a pan, saute cumin seeds, garlic and chopped methi leaves. Saute for some time and cool.

3. Add this to the chicken mince, also add garlic paste, egg yolk, grated cheese, chopped onion, green chilli, salt, red chilli powder, kebab chini powder, garam masala, and kasoori methi powder. Mix well.

Cooking

1. Divide this mixture into 16 equal parts and make balls.

2. Spread this mixture on the skewer using a moist palm along the length of the skewer in a cylindrical shape one inch apart and making each kebab 4 inches long.

3. Roast in a moderately hot tandoor or over a charcoal grill for 5-6 minutes. Baste with melted butter and further roast for 2-3 minutes.

4. Serve hot along with choice of salad and chutney.

TO SERVE: 4

COOKING TIME: 6-8 Minutes

Lamb Kebabs

▼

Lamb kebabs in particular are delicious. Tender, lean meat from the hind quarter, usually referred to as a prime cut, is best for kebabs. In addition to the two basic cuts, tikka and kebabs, that are common to poultry. Lamb has a number of other cuts that play an important role for tandoori food.

Bakra   :   Chunks of lamb with bone in the leg of lamb
              (1½" thickness, 100-110 gms).

Raan   :   Leg of kid lamb. Weight = 800-900 gms.

Rib Chop :   A chop is half an inch thick piece of meat with two bones.

Pasanda :   Flattened pieces of lamb, 4-5 inches long and ½ inch thick
              from hind leg of lamb.

         :   They are beaten and scored on one side in criss-cross pattern to
              facilitate tenderizing.

Tikka   :   2-inch cubes of lean meat from the hind leg of lamb.

Mince   :   Meat from the hind leg of lamb, free from fat and gristle minced.

Note : Before marinating, lamb meat should always be washed and drained
well with a kitchen towel and then placed into the marinade.

GOSHT PUDINA CHOP

▼

Ingredients

Mutton chop	-	16 nos
Raw papaya paste	-	for tenderizing
Fresh mint leaves	-	150 gm
Coriander leaves	-	50 gm
Green chillies	-	5 gm
Curry leaves	-	5 nos
Hung curd	-	100 ml
Cream	-	20 ml
Cashewnut paste	-	15 gm
Salt	-	to taste
Yellow chilli powder	-	1 tsp
Garam masala	-	1 tsp
Lemon juice	-	15 ml
Refined oil	-	25 ml
Melted butter	-	for basting

Method

1. Cut, clean and wash mutton chops. Give excisions/marks with a knife.

2. Apply raw papaya paste for tenderizing and leave it for some time.

3. In a prcessor, grind mint leaves, coriander leaves, green chillies, curry leaves to a smooth paste.

4. Remove extra papaya paste from the mutton chop and keep aside.

Marination

1. In a bowl take hung curd, add cream, cashewnut paste, garam masala, lemon juice and oil. Mix well.

2. Marinate the chops in above marinade and leave for 3-5 hours.

Cooking

1. In a skewer, leaving a gap of an inch, skew the marinated chops one by one. Roast in a moderatly hot tandoor or over a charcoal grill for about 12-15 minutes.

2. Remove and hang so that the excess moisture drain out completely (2-3 minutes).

3. Baste with clarified butter and further roast for 3–5 minutes.

4. Serve hot alongwith choice of salad and chutney.

TO SERVE: 4

COOKING TIME: 15-20 Minutes

GOSHT PUDINA CHOP

PASANDA KEBAB

▼

Ingredients

Lamb pasanda	-	1200 gm
Raw papaya paste	-	for tendering
Salt	-	to taste
White pepper powder	-	1 tsp
Ginger garlic paste	-	1 tbsp
Grated cottage cheese	-	150 gm
Egg white	-	1 no.
Cream	-	300 ml
Cashewnut paste	-	75 gm
White pepper powder	-	½ tbsp
Elachi powder	-	½ tsp
Kebab chini powder	-	½ tsp
Chopped green chilli (seedless)	-	20 gm
Melted butter	-	for basting

TO SERVE: 04

COOKING TIME: 12–15 Minutes

Method

Cut, clean lamb in pasanda cut; pat dry with a dry cloth.

First Marination

Apply raw papaya paste, salt, white pepper powder, ginger garlic to pasanda and keep aside for 1 hour.

Second Marination

1. In a deep tray, take grated cottage cheese, egg white and mix with palm. Add cream gradually and mix until it get blended. Add cashewnut paste and all the ingredients in decending order.

2. Marinate lamb pasanda in above marinade and keep aside for 2-3 hours.

Cooking

1. Take a skewer, skew marinated lamb one by one and roast in preheated tandoor or over charcoal grill for about 8-10 minutes.

2. Remove and hang so that the excess moisture drain out completely (1-2 minutes).

3. Baste with melted butter and further roast for about 3-5 minutes.

4. Remove and serve hot along with choice of salad or chutney.

ADRAKI CHAMPEN

▼

Ingredients

Mutton chop　　　　　-　16 nos.

First Marination

Raw papaya paste	-	for tenderizing
Ginger garlic paste	-	1 tbsp
Red chilli paste	-	1 tbsp
Ginger juice	-	1½ tbsp
Salt	-	to taste
Vinegar	-	10 ml
Refined oil	-	10 ml

Second Marination

Hung curd	-	300 ml
Ginger garlic paste	-	1 tbsp
Ginger juice	-	4 tbsp
Ginger (chopped)	-	60 gm
Salt	-	to taste
Garam masala	-	1 tbsp
Yellow chilli powder	-	3 tbsp
Kasoori methi powder	-	1 tsp
Refined oil	-	40 ml
Melted butter	-	for basting

Method

Clean, wash and pat dry the chops.

First Marination

Apply raw papaya paste and other ingredients to the lamb chops. Rub well and keep aside for 2-3 hours.

Second Marination

In a bowl whisk hung curd and add the remaining ingredients in the order listed. Mix well. Squeeze extra moisture from the marinated chops and put them in the above marinade. Keep aside for 3-4 hours.

Cooking

1. Take a skewer and skew the marinated lamb chops an inch apart by piercing from the meat and along the bone so that it does not fall.

2. Roast in tandoor or over a charcoal grill at a moderate temperature for 12-15 minutes.

3. Hang the skewer to let extra moisture drain out completely. Baste with melted butter and further roast for 4-6 minutes.

4. Serve hot with choice of salad and chutney.

TO SERVE: 4

COOKING TIME: 18-20 Minutes

▼

Ingredients

Tandoori mutton chops - 16 nos.

First Marination

Raw papaya paste	- for tenderizing
Ginger garlic paste	- 20 gm
Salt	- to taste
Red chilli paste	- 2 tbsp
Refined oil	- 10 ml

Second Marination

Hung curd	- 300 ml
Ginger garlic paste	- 20 gm
Red chilli paste	- 3 tbsp
Salt	- to taste
Garam masala	- ½ tbsp
Kasoori methi powder	- ½ tbsp
Lemon juice	- 10 ml
Mustard oil	- 25 ml
Melted butter	- for basting

Method

Take mutton chops and give incisions.

First Marination

Apply raw papaya paste, ginger garlic paste, salt, red chilli paste and refined oil to mutton chops and keep for 2 hours.

Second Marination

1. In a bowl take hung curd and add ginger garlic paste, red chilli paste, salt, garam masala, kasoori methi powder, lemon juice and mustard oil and mix.

2. Put chops in the above mixture, rub well and keep for 3-4 hours.

Cooking

1. Skewer the chops by piercing from the bottom towards the bone horizontally, one inch apart. Coat with remaining marinade.

2. Roast in a moderately hot tandoor for 12-15 minutes.

3. Remove and hang this skewer to let excess moisture drain out completely (2-3 minutes).

4. Baste with melted butter and roast for another 4-6 minutes.

5. Serve hot with choice of salad and chutney.

TO SERVE: 4

COOKING TIME: 18-20 Minutes

HUSSANI TANDOORI CHAMPEN

▼

Ingredients

Lamb chop - 16 nos.

First Marination

Raw papaya paste - for tenderizing

Ginger garlic paste - ½ tbsp

Salt - to taste

Yellow chilli powder - 1 tbsp

Vinegar - 10 ml

Refined oil - 10 ml

Second Marination

Cashewnut paste - 100 gm

Brown onion paste - 60 gm

Salt - to taste

Yellow chilli powder - 2 tbsp

Garam masala - 1 tbsp

Mint leaves (chopped) - 15 gm

Lemon juice - 25 ml

Refined oil - 40 ml

Melted butter - 30 ml

Method

Clean, wash and pat dry the lamb chop. Keep aside.

First Marination

Apply raw papaya, ginger garlic paste, salt, yellow chilli powder, vinegar, and oil to the lamb chop and rub well. Keep for 2 hours.

Second Marination

In a bowl take cashewnut paste and the remaining ingredients in the order listed. Mix well. Put the marinated lamb chops into this mixture. Rub well and leave to marinate for 3-4 hours.

Cooking

1. Take a skewer and skew the marinated lamb chops one inch apart by piercing from the meat and along the bone so that it does not fall.

2. Roast in a tandoor or over a charcoal grill at a moderate temperature for 12-15 minutes.

3. Hang the skewer to let the extra moisture drain out completely. Baste with melted butter and further roast for 4-6 minutes.

4. Serve hot with choice of salad and chutney.

TO SERVE: 4

COOKING TIME: 18-20 Minutes

▼

Ingredients

Mutton pasanda	-	16 pieces (75 gm each)

First Marination

Raw papaya paste	-	for tenderizing
Ginger garlic paste	-	1 tbsp
Red chilli paste	-	2 tbsp
Salt	-	to taste
Vinegar	-	20 ml
Refined oil	-	20 ml

Second Marination

Hung curd	-	200 ml
Brown onion paste	-	300 ml
Red chilli paste	-	2 tbsp
Ginger garlic paste	-	2 tbsp
Salt	-	to taste
Garam masala powder	-	2 tbsp
White pepper powder	-	1 tbsp
Lemon juice	-	60 ml
Refined oil	-	60 ml
Cloves	-	6 nos.
Ghee	-	20 ml
Melted butter	-	for basting

TO SERVE: 4

COOKING TIME: 12-15 Minutes

Method

Clean, then slightly flatten the mutton pieces with a steak hammer.

First Marination

Apply raw papaya paste, red chilli paste, salt, ginger garlic paste, vinegar, oil to the mutton pieces. Rub well and keep it for 1-2 hours.

Second Marination

1. In a bowl whisk hung curd and add the remaining ingredients in the order listed. Mix.

2. Remove extra moisture from the marinated mutton by lightly squeezing with hand. Put the mutton in the above marination and leave it for 3-4 hours.

3. Put the marinated mutton pieces in a pot. Put 3-4 pieces of burning charcoal in a small bowl along the mutton in pot. Put clove and pour ghee and immediately cover the pot with a lid for 3-5 minutes so that the smoke flavour penetrates into the mutton pieces.

Cooking

1. Take a skewer and skew the pasanda by piercing at both the ends, one inch apart. Coat with the remaining marinade.

2. Roast in a moderately hot tandoor for 10-12 minutes.

3. Remove and hang the skewer to allow the moisture to drain out completely (2-3 minutes).

4. Baste with melted butter and roast again for 3 minutes.

5. Serve hot along with choice of salad and chutney.

▼

Ingredients

Mutton boti	-	1 kg
Tomato	-	100 gm
Capsicum	-	100 gm
Onion	-	100 gm

First Marination

Raw papaya paste	-	for tenderizing
Ginger garlic paste	-	1 tbsp
Red chilli paste	-	1½ tbsp
Salt	-	to taste
Garam masala	-	½ tbsp
Vinegar	-	10 ml
Refined oil	-	10 ml

Second Marination

Hung curd	-	300 gm
Ginger garlic paste	-	1 tbsp
Red chilli paste	-	2 tbsp
Salt	-	to taste
Garam masala	-	1 tbsp
Kasoori methi powder	-	½ tbsp
Lemon juice	-	20 ml
Refined oil	-	40 ml
Melted butter	-	30 ml

Method

1. Clean, wash and pat dry the mutton boti.

2. Cut tomato into 4 pieces, deseed. Cut capsicum into 4 pieces and deseed. Peel and cut onion into 4 pieces. Cut all the items into large cubes and keep aside.

First Marination

Apply raw papaya paste, ginger garlic paste, red chilli paste, salt, garam masala, vinegar, and refined oil to the mutton boti. Rub well and keep it for 2-3 hours.

Second Marination

1. Whisk hung curd in a bowl and add the remaining ingredients in the order listed. Mix.

2. Remove extra moisture from the marinated boti and put it in the above marinade. Leave for 3-4 hours.

Cooking

1. Take a skewer and skew marinated mutton pieces and vegetable alternately along the skewer lengthwise. Roast in a tandoor or over a charcoal grill at a moderate temperature for 10-12 minutes.

2. Remove and hang so the excess moisture drains out completely (2-3 minutes). Baste with melted butter and further roast for 3-4 minutes.

3. Serve hot along with choice of salad and chutney.

TO SERVE: 4

COOKING TIME: 12-15 Minutes

RAJASTHANI BOTI KEBAB

▼

Ingredients

Mutton boti — 1 kg
(20 pieces)

First Marination

Raw papaya paste	-	for tenderizing
Ginger garlic paste	-	1 tbsp
Red chilli paste	-	1 tbsp
Salt	-	to taste
Vinegar	-	20 ml
Refined oil	-	20 ml

Second Marination

Hung curd	-	300 ml
Ginger garlic paste	-	1½ tbsp
Red chilli paste	-	3 tbsp
Garam masala	-	1 tbsp
Kasoori methi powder	-	½ tbsp
Salt	-	to taste
Lemon juice	-	25 ml
Mustard oil	-	40 ml
Melted butter	-	30 ml

TO SERVE: 4

COOKING TIME: 12-15 Minutes

Method

Wash and pat dry mutton pieces.

First Marination

Apply raw papaya paste, ginger garlic paste, red chilli paste, salt, vinegar, and oil to mutton boti and mix. Rub well and keep aside for 1-2 hours.

Second Marination

1. In a bowl whisk hung curd and add the remaining ingredients in the order listed. Mix well.

2. Remove excess moisture from the marinated mutton pieces and put them in the above marinade. Leave for 2-3 hours.

Cooking

1. Take a skewer and skew marinated pieces one inch apart along the skewer.

2. Roast in a tandoor or over a charcoal grill at a moderate temperature for 10-12 minutes.

3. Hang the skewer to let extra moisture drain out completely (2-3 minutes).

4. Baste with melted butter and further roast for 3-4 minutes.

5. Serve hot along with choice of salad and chutney.

▼

Ingredients

Mutton mince (fine)	-	800 gm
Ginger garlic paste	-	1 tsp
Cashewnut paste	-	3 tbsp
Khus khus paste	-	1 tbsp
Salt	-	to taste
Garam masala	-	1 tbsp
Yellow chilli powder	-	1 tbsp
Ghee	-	20 gm
Melted butter	-	for basting

Method

1. In a tray take mutton mince, add ginger garlic paste and all the ingredients as listed.

2. Divide the mixture in to 16 equal parts and make balls.

3. Take a skewer and using a moist hand apply each ball on the skewer in a cylindrical shape along the skewer. Grill over charcoal grill at a moderate temperature for 4-6 minutes.

4. Baste with melted butter and further roast for 1-2 minutes.

5. Serve hot along with choice of salad and chutney.

TO SERVE: 4

COOKING TIME: 6-8 Minutes

SEEKH GILAFI

▼

Ingredients

Mutton mince	-	600 gm
Ginger garlic paste	-	2 tbsp
Onion (chopped)	-	4 tbsp
Chopped spring onion (green)	-	6 tbsp
Tomato (chopped)	-	4 tbsp
Capsicum (chopped)	-	4 tbsp
Green chilly (chopped)	-	2 tbsp
Coriander (chopped)	-	3 tbsp
Kashmiri red chilli powder	-	2 tbsp
Kebab chini powder	-	a pinch
Garam masala	-	2 tbsp
Lemon juice	-	2 tbsp
Salt	-	to taste
Melted butter	-	30 ml

Method

1. In a bowl take mutton mince, ginger garlic paste, 2 tbsp each of chopped onion, tomato, capsicum, reserving the balance for later use.

2. Add all the remaining ingredients in the order listed, rub well with your palm, and correct seasoning.

3. Divide this mixture into 16 equal portions and make balls.

Cooking

1. Spread this mixture on the skewer using a wet hand to press each ball along the length of the skewer in a cylindrical shape, one inch apart and making each kebab 4 inches long. Apply the remaining chopped vegetables on each seekh. Spread evenly.

2. Roast in a moderately hot tandoor or over churcoal grill for 5-6 minutes.

3. Remove and hang so that the excess moisture drains out completely (2-3 minutes).

4. Baste with melted butter and further roast for 2-3 minutes.

5. Serve hot along with choice of salad and chutney.

TO SERVE: 4

COOKING TIME: 6-8 Minutes

NOORANI SEEKH

▼

Ingredients

Mutton mince	-	400 gm
Ginger (chopped)	-	5 gm
Onion (chopped)	-	25 gm
Coriander (chopped)	-	10 gm
Ginger garlic paste	-	5 gm
Red chilli paste	-	15 gm
Salt	-	to taste
Garam masala	-	½ tsp
Kasoori methi	-	½ tsp
Oil	-	50 ml
Chicken mince	-	400 gm
Grated cheese	-	40 gm
Cream	-	40 ml
Ginger garlic paste	-	10 gm
Chopped green chilli (seedless)	-	2 gm
Salt	-	to taste
Elaichi javitri powder	-	a pinch
White pepper powder	-	½ tsp
Melted butter	-	for basting

TO SERVE: 4

COOKING TIME: 8-10 Minutes

Method

Mutton Mince

1. Take mutton mince in a deep tray.
2. Add chopped ginger, onion, coriander, add ginger garlic paste, red chilli paste, salt, garam masala, kasoori methi and oil.
3. Mix it with your palm and keep aside for 30 minutes.

Chicken Mince

1. Take chicken mince in a deep tray.
2. Add grated cheese, cream, ginger garlic paste and mix thoroughly with your palm. Add chopped green chilli, salt, elaichi javitri powder, white pepper powder and mix. Keep aside for 30 minutes.

Cooking

1. Divide both the marinated mince into 16 equal portions and make balls.
2. Spread this mixture on the skewer by pressing each ball along the length of the skewer in a cylindrical shape one inch apart, making each kebab 4 inches long.
3. In the same manner spread chicken mince on top of the lamb mince kebab and roll it into a cylindrical shape.
4. Roast in a moderately hot tandoor for 5-6 minutes.
5. Remove and hang the skewer to allow the excess moisture to drains out completely (2-3 minutes).
6. Baste it with melted butter and further roast for 2-3 minutes.
7. Transfer to a serving plate. Cut into desired pieces diagnoally and serve hot with choice of salads and chutney.

SEEKH KEBAB

▼

Ingredients

Mutton mince	-	800 gm
Ginger (chopped)	-	10 gm
Onion (chopped)	-	50 gm
Mint (chopped)	-	10 gm
Coriander (chopped)	-	20 gm
Ginger garlic paste	-	15 gm
Red chilli paste	-	25 gm
Salt	-	to taste
Garam masala	-	1 tsp
Kasoori methi	-	½ tsp
Refined oil	-	10 ml
Melted butter	-	for basting

Method

1. Take mutton mince in a deep tray.

2. Add chopped ginger, onion, mint, coriander to the mince.

3. Add ginger garlic paste, red chilli paste, salt, garam masala, kasoori methi and oil.

4. Mix with your palm and keep aside for 30 minutes.

Cooking

1. Divide mince mixture into 16 equal portions and make balls.

2. Spread this mixture on the skewer, using a wet palm to press each ball along the length of the skewer in a cylindrical shape, one inch apart and making each kebab 4 inches long.

3. Roast in a moderately hot tandoor or over a charcoal grill for 5-6 minutes. Baste it with melted butter and further roast for 2-3 minutes.

4. Transfer on to a plate and serve hot with choice of salad and chutney.

TO SERVE: 4

COOKING TIME: 6-8 Minutes

▼

Ingredients

Eggs	-	8 nos
Mutton mince	-	400 gm
Ginger garlic paste	-	10 gm
Cashewnut paste	-	15 gm
Grated processed cheese	-	20 gm
Egg yolk	-	1 no.
Onion (chopped)	-	30 gm
Ginger (chopped)	-	15 gm
Green chilli (chopped)	-	10 gm
Coriander (chopped)	-	20 gm
Salt	-	to taste
Kashmiri red chilli powder	-	½ tbsp
Garam masala	-	1½ tbsp
Chaat masala	-	2 tbsp
Saffron	-	a pinch
Gram flour roasted	-	3 tbsp
Cornflour	-	3 tbsp
Refined oil	-	2 tbsp
Melted butter	-	30 ml

Method

1. Hard boil the eggs, deshell and keep aside.

2. In a bowl take mutton mince and add the remaining ingredients in the order listed. Rub well. Correct seasoning.

3. Divide this into 8 equal portions and make balls.

4. Flatten each ball on a wet palm. Place a boiled egg on the flattened mince and cover it with mince. Seal, shape it with a moist/oily hand and keep it in a freezer for 2 hours.

Cooking

1. Take a skewer and skew each egg one inch apart. Roast in a tandoor at a moderate temperature for 6-8 minutes.

2. Baste with melted butter. Remove and cut each egg into half. Sprinkle chaat masala.

3. Serve hot along with choice of salad and chutney.

TO SERVE: 4

COOKING TIME: 6-8 Minutes

SHAMMI KEBAB

▼

Ingredients

Mutton mince	-	I kg
Chana dal	-	100 gm
Black cardamom	-	3 nos.
Green cardamom	-	5 nos.
Red chilli (whole)	-	5 nos.
Black peppercorn	-	5 gm
Salt	-	to taste
Turmeric	-	½ tsp
Coriander (chopped)	-	30 gm
Green chilli (chopped)	-	15 gm
Refined oil	-	for frying

Method

1. In a pan take mutton mince, chana dal, black and green cardamom, red chilly whole, black peppercorn, salt, turmeric. Add water and cook all ingredients on slow fire until done and water gets evaporated.

2. Remove whole condiments and cool.

3. In a processor put the mince and make a fine paste. Transfer mince to a bowl, add chopped coriander and green chilli and mix.

Cooking

1. Divide this mixture into 20 equal portions and make balls. Apply a little melted ghee in your palm and flatten the mince ball into a round medallion (tikki) shape (2-2½" diameter).

2. Heat oil in a pan and deep fry until golden brown and crisp on both sides.

3. Serve hot along with choice of salad and chutney.

TO SERVE: 4

COOKING TIME: 2-3 Minutes

SIKHAMPURI KEBAB

▼

Ingredients

Mutton mince	-	1 kg
Chana dal	-	100 gm
Black cardamom	-	3 nos.
Green cardamom	-	5 nos.
Red chilli whole	-	5 nos.
Black peppercorn	-	5 gm
Salt	-	to taste
Turmeric	-	½ tsp
Coriander (chopped)	-	30 gm
Green chilli (chopped)	-	15 gm
Refined oil	-	for frying

Stuffing

Onion (chopped)	-	50 gm
Chopped boiled egg whites	-	2 nos.
Salt	-	to taste
Crushed peppercorn	-	1 tsp

Method

1. In a pan take mutton mince, chana dal, black and green cardamom, red chilli whole, black peppercorn, salt and turmeric. Add water and cook all ingredients on slow fire until done and water gets evaporated.

2. Remove whole condiments and cool.

3. In a processor put the mince and make a fine paste. Transfer mince to a bowl, add chopped coriander and green chilli and mix.

Stuffing

1. In a bowl mix chopped onion, chopped egg whites, salt, and crushed black peppercorn.

2. Divide this cooked mixture into 20 equal portions and make balls. Place a portion of stuffing in the middle, seal carefully and make balls. Flatten into a round pattern.

Cooking

1. Heat oil in a pan and deep fry until golden brown and crisp on both sides.

2. Serve hot along with choice of salad and chutney.

TO SERVE: 4

COOKING TIME: 2-3 Minutes

MUTHIYA KEBAB

▼

Ingredients

Lamb mince	-	800 gms
Lamb fat	-	50 gms
Onion (chopped)	-	75 gms
Ginger (chopped)	-	15 gms
Green chilli (chopped)	-	10 gms
Garlic (chopped)	-	10 gms.
Coriander (chopped)	-	05 gms
Mint (chopped)	-	05 gms
Salt	-	to taste

Method

1. Take lamb mince in a bowl, Add all the above ingredients in the order listed. Mix well until thoroughly blended and forms a smooth consistency.

2. Divide the mixture Into 16 equal parts/balls, making each portion of 50 gms.

Cooking

1. Apply each ball on skewer horizonally using a moist palm giving a *muthi* shape (3" long).

2. Roast in moderately hot tandoor or over charcoal Grill for about 5-6 minutes untill half done.

3. Remove and hang to let the excess moisture drain out completely (2-3 minutes).

4. Baste with clarified butter and further roast in a tandoor/charcoal grill for 4-5 minutes.

5. Remove and serve hot with choice of salad and chutney.

TO SERVE: 4

COOKING TIME: 10-12 Minutes

▼

GALOUTI KEBAB

▼

Ingredients

Mutton mince (fine)	-	800 gm
Ginger garlic paste	-	1 tsp
Cashewnut paste	-	3 tbsp
Khus khus paste	-	1 tbsp
Salt	-	to taste
Garam masala	-	1 tbsp
Yellow chilli powder	-	1 tbsp
Cloves	-	6 nos
Ghee	-	20 gm
Refined oil	-	50 ml

Method

1. In a bowl take mutton mince, add ginger garlic paste, cashewnut paste, khus khus paste, salt, garam masala and yellow chilli powder and mix well. Keep it for 30 minutes.

2. Put mince in a bowl. Put 3-4 pieces of burning charcoal in a small bowl along the mince in the bowl. Put cloves and pour ghee and immediately cover the bowl with a lid for 3-5 minutes.

3. Divide this mixture into 16 equal portions and make balls. Apply a little melted ghee on your palm and flatten the mince balls into round patties or medallion shape (tikki).

Cooking

1. Heat ghee on a pan and shallow fry over low heat until both sides are evenly brown and crisp.

2. Serve hot with choice of salad and chutney.

TO SERVE: 4

COOKING TIME: 2-3 Minutes

GALOUTI KEBAB
▼

▼

▼

Ingredients

Raan (lamb leg)   -   I kg

First Marination

Raw papaya paste	-	for tenderizing
Cinnamon powder	-	¼ tbsp
Cardamom powder	-	I tsp
Clove powder	-	I tsp
Aniseed powder	-	I tsp
Cumin powder	-	I tsp
Coriander powder	-	2 tbsp
Nutmeg powder	-	½ tsp
Ginger powder	-	I tbsp

Second Marination

Hung curd	-	300 ml
Garlic paste	-	100 gm
Green paste	-	2 tbsp
Red chilli paste	-	30 gm
Garlic (chopped)	-	30 gm
Salt	-	to taste
Turmeric	-	½ tbsp
Kebab chini powder	-	2 pinches
Lemon juice	-	50 ml
Refined oil	-	100 ml
Melted butter	-	30 ml

TO SERVE: 4

COOKING TIME: 45-55 Minutes

Method

Clean and remove the blade bone of the leg, giving incisions all over.

First Marination

In a bowl take raw papaya paste, crushed cinnamon, cardamom, clove, aniseeds, cumin, coriander, nutmeg powder, and ginger powder and apply this to the raan. Rub well and leave for 2-3 hours.

Second Marination

Whisk hung curd in a bowl and put the remaining ingredients in the order listed. Mix. Remove extra moisture from the marinated raan and put it in this marinade. Rub well and keep aside for 2-3 hours.

Cooking

1. Take a thick bottomed pan/tray and place the raan along with entire marinade.

2. In a preheated oven roast raan till ¾ cooked and remove.

3. Cut raan into 3-4 pieces along the bone.

4. Take a skewer and skew raan pieces and further roast in a tandoor at a moderate temperature for 6-8 minutes.

5. Baste with melted butter and further roast for 3-4 minutes.

6. Slice raan, arrange on a platter and serve hot along with choice of salad and chutney.

Sea Food

▼

Man is thought to have caught, prepared and eaten fresh and marine-water fish much before he domesticated animals. Today fish is an important part of most kitchens of the world. There are large varieties of edible sea and fresh-water fish that are known and available in India. Sole, Mali, Surmai, Pomfret, Betki, Singhara, White Salmon, Rahu are the ones used most often in Indian food preparations.

Fish being low in fat and high in water content is very delicate. For best results in cooking of fish follow the given tips:

1. Use absolutely fresh fish.

2. Cooking time should be kept to minimum as the fish gets dry when over-cooked.

3. Temperature should remain low while cooking fish to give the right texture.

4. Basting should be done a couple of times to keep the fish moist.

5. Cooking time is allotted by the type of cut and size being used.

6. Deodorizing and skewing the fish in the correct way are the most important features.

The types of cuts used for tandoori cooking are:

Whole Fish   : Medium-sized fish Pomfret (400–450 gms) or Trout (250–275 gms).

Tikka   : 2-2½ inch boneless pieces.

Mince   : Fresh mince can be made by taking thick fillets of fish.

Lobster   : A rare delicacy — fresh lobster tails. Usually 100-125 gms each are recommended.

Fresh Prawn : Medium sized prawn tails approx. (75–90 gms) each with tail.

DARIYA KA RATAN

▼

Ingredients
Fresh prawn
(large 50-60 gm each)   -   20 nos.

First Marination
Lemon juice	-	20 ml
Ginger garlic paste	-	1 tbsp
Salt	-	to taste
Yellow chilli powder	-	1 tsp
Ajwain	-	1 tsp
Turmeric powder	-	1 tsp

Second Marination
Hung curd	-	300 gm
Ginger garlic paste	-	1 tbsp
Salt	-	to taste
Yellow chilli powder	-	1 tbsp
Garam masala	-	½ tbsp
Roasted chana powder	-	1 tbsp
Mustard oil	-	100 ml
Ajwain	-	2 tbsp
Turmeric powder	-	1 tsp
Melted butter	-	for basting

TO SERVE: 4

COOKING TIME: 10-12 Minutes

Method
Remove the shell and the vein of the prawn and wash thoroughly.

First Marination
1. Rub prawns with lemon juice, ginger garlic paste, salt, yellow chilli powder, ajwain, and turmeric. Keep for 30 minutes.

Second Marination
1. Whisk hung curd in a bowl, add ginger garlic paste, salt, garam masala, yellow chilli powder, roasted chana powder. Mix well.

2. Heat mustard oil in a pan and remove from fire. Add ajwain and turmeric and immediately add this to the above mixture and mix well.

3. After removing excess moisture, put marinated prawns in this mixture. Rub well and keep aside for 2 hours.

Cooking
1. Take a skewer and skew marinated prawns one by one an inch apart, coating with remaining marinade.

2. Roast in a moderately hot tandoor or over a charcoal grill for 8-10 minutes.

3. Remove and hang the skewer to allow excess moisture to drain out completely (2-3 minutes).

4. Baste with melted butter and roast again for 2-3 minutes.

5. Transfer to a plate and serve hot with choice of salad and chutney.

▼

Ingredients

Prawns (B grade)	-	150 gm
Crab beat	-	100 gm
Pomfret fish fillet	-	150 gm
Betki fish fillet	-	400 gm
Salt	-	to taste
Curry leaves	-	2-3 nos.
Lemon juice	-	10 ml
Onions (chopped)	-	75 gm
Coriander (chopped)	-	20 gm
Ginger (chopped)	-	15 gm
Green Chilli (chopped)	-	15 gm
Red Chilli Powder	-	½ tbsp
White Pepper	-	½ tbsp

Preparation

1. Clean and devein prawns, crab meat, cut pomfret and betki into small pieces.

2. In a bowl boil water and add salt, curry leaves, lemon juice, add above seafood for some time and drain it and cool.

3. Mince all the seafood. Add chopped onions, coriander, ginger, green chillies, salt, red chilli powder, white pepper and mix thoroughly. Keep aside.

Cooking

1. Divide this mixture into 16 equal portions and make balls.

2. Take a skewer, apply this mixture on skewer in a cylindrical shape (4") and roast in a moderately hot tandoor or over a charcoal grill for 5-6 minutes.

3. Remove and hang so that the excess moisture drains out completely (1-2 minutes).

4. Baste with clarified butter and further roast it for 2-3 minutes.

5. Remove and serve hot along with choice of salad and chutney.

TO SERVE: 4

COOKING TIME: 6-8 Minutes

TANDOORI LOBSTER

▼

Ingredients

Lobster   -   8 nos.

First Marination

Ginger garlic paste	-	1 tbsp
Red chilli paste	-	1 tbsp
Salt	-	to taste
Vinegar	-	10 ml
Refined oil	-	10 ml

Second Marination

Hung curd	-	300 ml
Ginger garlic paste	-	½ tbsp
Red chilli paste	-	1 tbsp
Salt	-	to taste
Ajwain	-	½ tbsp
Garam masala	-	1 tbsp
Kasoori methi powder	-	½ tbsp
Mustard oil	-	40 ml
Melted butter	-	for basting

Method

Deshell, devein the lobster retaining its tail. Wash, pat dry and keep aside.

First Marination

In a bowl take ginger garlic paste, red chilly paste, salt, vinegar, and refined oil and mix. Apply this mixture to lobster tails. Rub well and keep for 1 hour.

Second Marination

1. In a bowl whisk hung curd, add the remaining ingredients and mix.

2. Squeeze excess moisture from lobster tail and dip in the above mixture. Rub well and keep for 1-2 hours.

Cooking

1. Take a skewer and skew marinated lobster from tail to head on both sides. Apply the remaining mixture on them.

2. Roast in tandoor or over a charcoal grill at a moderate temperature for 8-10 minutes.

3. Remove and hang skewer to let excess moisture drain out completely.

4. Baste with melted butter and further roast it for 2-4 minutes.

5. Serve hot along with choice of salad and chutney.

TO SERVE: 4

COOKING TIME: 10-12 Minutes

KASOORI JHINGA

▼

Ingredients

Prawn tail (A grade) 50-60 gm	-	20 nos.
Curry leaves	-	10 gm
Coriander leaves	-	50 gm
Mint leaves	-	10 gm
Green chilly	-	5 gm
Ginger garlic paste	-	30 gm
Salt	-	to taste
Kasoori methi powder	-	60 gm
Lemon juice	-	30 ml
Hung curd	-	300 ml
Cream	-	50 ml
Egg	-	1 no.
Kashmiri red chilli powder	-	2 tsp
Ajwain	-	½ tsp
Garam masala	-	½ tsp
Cornflour	-	20 gm
Refined oil	-	80 ml
Melted butter	-	for basting

TO SERVE: 4

COOKING TIME: 10-12 Minutes

Method

1. Deshell, devein and clean the prawn retaining the tail. Pat dry and keep aside.

2. In a blender put curry leaves, coriander leaves, mint leaves, green chilli and make a fine paste. Transfer to a bowl.

First Marination

1. In a bowl take ½ ginger garlic paste, salt, ½ of kasoori methi powder, lemon juice, mix thoroughly and apply it to the prawn. Rub well and keep for ½ hours.

Second Marination

1. In a bowl whisk hung curd, add the green paste and all the remaining ingredients in the order listed. Mix well.

2. Squeeze excess moisture from the prawn and put it in the above marination. Rub well and keep aside for 1½ -2 hours.

Cooking

1. Take a skewer and skew marinated prawns from tail to head on both sides. Apply the remaining mixture on them.

2. Roast in tandoor or over a charcoal grill at a moderate temperature for 8-10 minutes.

3. Remove and hang skewer to let excess moisture drain out completely.

4. Baste with clarified butter and further roast it for 2-3 minutes.

5. Serve hot along with choice of salad and chutney.

▼

Ingredients

Pomfret (350-400 gm)	-	4 nos
Ginger garlic paste	-	30 gm
Yellow chilly paste	-	1 tbsp
Salt	-	to taste
Lemon juice	-	30 ml
Ajwain	-	1 tbsp
Hung curd	-	350 gm
Egg	-	1 no.
Turmeric powder	-	½ tbsp
Ajwain powder	-	1 tsp
Garam masala	-	1 tbsp
Roasted gram flour	-	50 ml
Mustard oil	-	45 ml
Melted butter	-	for basting

Method

Clean, slightly trim fins, tail, wash and give incisions (3-4) on both sides. Pat dry and keep aside.

First Marination

In a bowl take ½ of the ginger garlic paste, ½ yellow chilli paste, salt, lemon juice, and ajwain. Apply this mixture to pomfret. Rub well and keep it for ½ hours.

Second Marination

1. In a bowl whisk hung curd, add the remaining ingredients in the order listed and mix.

2. Squeeze excess moisture from the pomfret and dip it in the above marination. Rub well and keep for 1½-2 hours.

Cooking

1. Take a skewer, skew marinated pomfret from mouth to tail 2 inches apart. Apply the remaining marinade. Roast it in a tandoor at a moderate temperature for 7-8 minutes.

2. Remove and hang skewer upright to let the excess moisture drain out completely (3-4 minutes).

3. Baste with melted butter and further roast for 3-4 minutes.

4. Serve hot along with choice of salad and chutney.

TO SERVE: 4

COOKING TIME: 10-12 Minutes

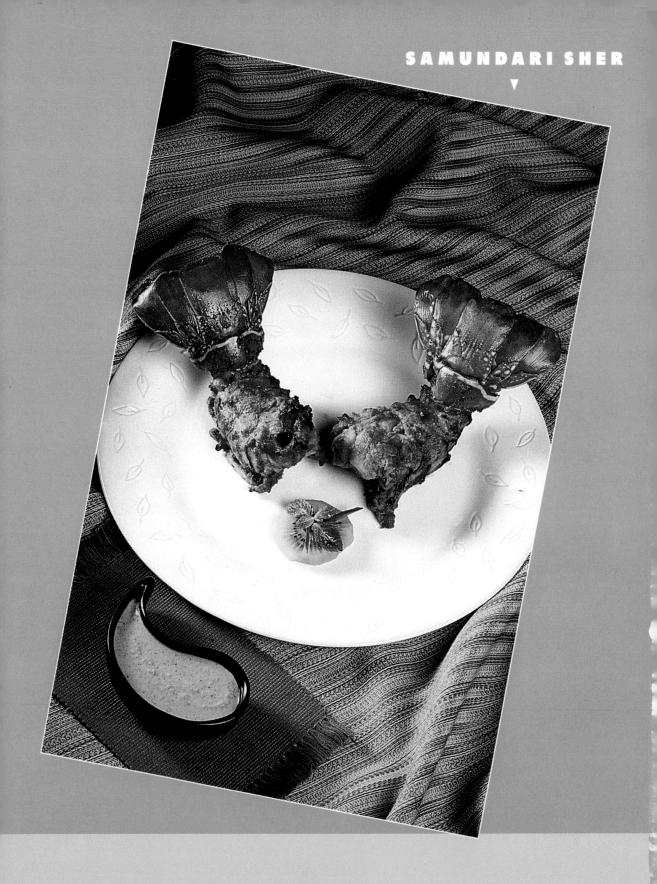

▼

Ingredients

Lobster tail (100-125 gm)	-	8 pieces
Hung curd	-	300 ml
Ginger garlic paste	-	15 gm
Egg	-	2 nos.
Sesame seed paste	-	30 gm
Salt	-	to taste
Kashmiri red chilli powder	-	3 tbsp
Garam masala	-	1 tbsp
Ajwain	-	2 tbsp
Kalonji	-	2 tbsp
Turmeric powder	-	¼ tbsp
Raw mango powder	-	1 tbsp
Mustard powder	-	a pinch
Roasted gram flour	-	2 tbsp
Lemon juice	-	20 ml
Mustard oil	-	100 ml
Melted butter	-	for basting

Method

Deshell, devein the lobster retaining the tail. Wash, pat dry and keep aside.

Marination

In a bowl whisk hung curd, add the remaining ingredients in the order listed. Mix thoroughly. Put lobster tail into this mixture, rub well and keep aside for 1½-2 hours.

Cooking

1. Take a skewer and skew marinated lobster from tail to head on both sides. Apply the remaining mixture on them.

2. Roast in a tandoor or over a charcoal grill at a moderate temperature for 8-10 minutes.

3. Remove and hang skewer to let excess moisture drain out completely (2-3 minutes).

4. Baste with melted butter and further roast it for 2-3 minutes.

5. Serve hot along with choice of salad and chutney.

TO SERVE: 4

COOKING TIME: 10-12 Minutes

▼

Ingredients

Prawns A Grade (50-60 gm)	-	20 nos.
Hung curd	-	400 gm
Salt	-	to taste
Yellow chilli powder	-	½ tbsp
Ginger powder	-	1 tsp
Ginger (chopped)	-	20 gm
Lemon juice	-	15 ml
Ginger juice	-	½ tbsp
Mustard oil	-	40 ml
Turmeric	-	½ tbsp
Melted butter	-	for basting

Method

Deshell, devein the prawns retaining the tail. Wash, pat dry and keep aside.

Marination

1. In a bowl whisk hung curd, add salt, yellow chilli powder, ginger powder, chopped ginger, lemon juice and ginger juice. Mix well.

2. Heat mustard oil in a pan (till smoking point). Add turmeric to it and add this to the curd mixture. Cover the bowl with a lid for 2 minutes. Mix well.

3. Marinate prawns in this marinade for ½ hours.

Cooking

1. Take a skewer and skew marinated prawns from tail to head on both sides. Apply the remaining mixture on them.

2. Roast in a tandoor or over a charcoal grill at a moderate temperature for 8-10 minutes.

3. Remove and hang skewer to let excess moisture drain out completely.

4. Baste with melted butter and further roast it for 2-3 minutes.

5. Serve hot along with choice of salad and chutney.

TO SERVE: 4

COOKING TIME: 10-12 Minutes

JHINGA NISHA

▼

Ingredients

Prawns A grade (50-60 gm)	-	20 nos.
Hung curd	-	300 ml
Cream	-	30 ml
Ginger garlic paste	-	15 gm
Egg	-	1 no.
Grated processed cheese	-	30 gm
Onion (chopped)	-	20 gm
Ginger (chopped)	-	5 gm
Coriander (chopped)	-	25 gm
Mint leaves (chopped)	-	10 gm
Salt	-	to taste
Kasoori methi powder	-	1 tsp
Clove powder	-	½ tsp
Dalchini powder	-	1 tsp
Tandoori masala	-	1 tbsp
Melted butter	-	for basting

Method

Deshell and devein the prawns retaining the tail. Wash, pat dry and keep aside.

Marination

In a bowl whisk hung curd and add all the ingredients in the order listed. Mix well. Put prawn tail into this marinade. Rub well and keep for 2 hours.

Cooking

1. Take a skewer and skew marinated prawns from tail to head on both sides. Apply the remaining mixture on them.

2. Roast in a tandoor or over a charcoal grill at moderate temperature for 8-10 minutes.

3. Remove and hang skewer to let excess moisture drain out completely.

4. Baste with melted butter and further roast it for 2-3 minutes.

5. Serve hot along with choice of salad and chutney.

TO SERVE: 4

COOKING TIME: 10-12 Minutes

TANDOORI LAL MOTI TIKKA

▼

Ingredients

Prawn tail		
(small size-30 gm)	-	40 nos.
Hung curd	-	200 ml
Cream	-	50 ml
Egg	-	I no.
Mint chutney	-	40 gm
Semolina (roasted)	-	15 gm
Salt	-	to taste
Turmeric	-	a pinch
Kashmiri red chilli powder	-	I tbsp
Clove powder	-	I tsp
Cinnamon powder	-	I tsp
Bayleaf powder	-	I tsp
Raw mango powder	-	I tsp
Mustard powder	-	½ tsp
Ajwain	-	I tsp
Crushed anardana	-	I tbsp
Lemon juice	-	20 ml
Refined oil	-	80 ml
Melted butter	-	for basting

Method

Deshell, devein, wash and pat dry tiger prawn. Keep aside.

Marination

In a bowl whisk hung curd and add all the ingredients in the order listed. Mix. Put prawn into this marinade. Rub well and keep aside for 2 hours.

Cooking

1. Take a skewer and skew marinated prawns from tail to head from both sides. Apply the remaining mixture on them.

2. Roast in a tandoor or over a charcoal grill at moderate temperature for 2-4 minutes.

3. Remove and hang skewer to let excess moisture drain out completely.

4. Baste with melted butter and further roast it for 2-3 minutes.

5. Serve hot along with choice of salad and chutney.

TO SERVE: 4

COOKING TIME: 6-8 Minutes

▼

JALPARI KEBAB

▼

Ingredients

Prawn tail A grade
(50-60 gm) - 8 nos.
Fish fillet (50-60 gm) - 8 nos.

Marination of Prawns

Ginger garlic paste - 30 gm
Red chilli paste - 40 gm
Salt - to taste
Ajwain - 20 gm
Hung curd - 200 ml
Cream - 60 ml
Egg - 1 no.
Turmeric - 1 tbsp
Ajwain seed - 2 tbsp
Garam masala - 1 tsp
Lemon juice - 25 ml
Refined oil - 60 ml

Marination of Fish

Ginger garlic paste - 30 gm
Salt - to taste
Ajwain - 20 gm
Hung curd - 200 ml
Cream - 60 ml
Egg - 1 no.
Ajwain seed - 2 tbsp
Garam masala - 1 tsp
Lemon juice - 25 ml
Refined oil - 60 ml
Melted butter - for basting

TO SERVE: 4

COOKING TIME: 10-12 Minutes

Method

1. Deshell and devein prawn tail. Wash, pat dry and keep aside.
2. Flatten fish fillet ¼ inch, trim the sides so that a prawn can be rolled in each fillet.

Marination of Prawns

First Marination

Apply half of the ginger garlic paste and red chilli paste, salt, ajwain to the prawn. Rub well and keep for ½ hours.

Second Marination

1. In a bowl whisk hung curd and add the remaining ingredients in the order listed and mix.
2. Squeeze excess moisture from the prawn and put it in the above marinade. Keep for 1½ to 2 hours.

Marination of Fish

Prepare marination same as for prawns except for red chilli powder and turmeric powder. Arrange fish fillet on a tray. Apply marinade on the fish on both sides. Keep it for 1½ to 2 hours.

Cooking

1. Take marinated fillets and place marinated prawn tail on it, roll and secure it with a toothpick at the end.
2. Prepare all the fillets in the same way and keep aside.
3. Take a skewer and skew marinated fish and prawn roll one inch apart, cover with the remaining marinade. Roast it in a tandoor at a moderate temperature for 8-10 minutes.
4. Remove and hang skewer to let excess moisture drain out completely (2-3 minutes).
5. Baste with melted butter and further roast for 3-4 minutes.
6. Serve hot with choice of salad and chutney.

TANDOORI TROUT

▼

Ingredients

Trout   - 4 nos.
                         (250-275 gm each)

First Marination

Salt	- to taste
Yellow chilli powder	- 1 tsp
Ginger garlic powder	- ½ tbsp
Lemon juice	- 10 ml

Second Marination

Hung curd	- 350 ml
Ginger garlic paste	- 1 tbsp
Salt	- to taste
Yellow chilli powder	- 1½ tbsp
Ajwain	- ½ tsp
Garam masala	- 1 tsp
Mustard oil	- 45 ml
Turmeric	- ½ tbsp
Melted butter	- for basting

Method

Cut, clean and wash the fish. Make 4 deep incisions across each side. Pat dry and keep aside.

First Marination

In a bowl mix salt, yellow chilli powder, ginger garlic paste and lemon juice. Apply this to the fish and keep it for ½ hours.

Second Marination

1. In a bowl whisk hung curd, add ginger garlic paste, salt, yellow chilli powder, ajwain and garam masala. Mix and keep aside.

2. Heat mustard oil in a pan, add turmeric to it and add this oil to the above marinade. Cover it with a lid for 2 minutes then mix.

3. Remove excess moisture from the fish by lightly squeezing it with your palm and dip it in the above marinade. Leave it for 1 hour.

Cooking

1. Take a skewer and skew the fish from mouth to tail carefully without breaking it from the centre. Roast it in a moderate tandoor for 7-8 minutes.

2. Remove and hang the skewer to let excess moisture drain out completely (2-3 minutes).

3. Baste with melted butter and further roast for 3-4 minutes.

4. Remove and serve hot with choice of salad and chutney.

TO SERVE: 4

COOKING TIME: 10-12 Minutes

MAHI TIKKA AJWAINI

▼

Ingredients

Fish fillet	-	I kg
Hung curd	-	300 gm

First Marination

Lemon juice	-	20 ml
Ginger garlic paste	-	2 tbsp
Salt	-	to taste
Yellow chilli powder	-	I tbsp
Ajwain	-	2 tbsp
Turmeric powder	-	I tbsp

Second Marination

Garam masala powder	-	½ tbsp
Roasted chana powder	-	I tbsp
Mustard oil	-	45 ml
Melted butter	-	for basting

Method

Trim and cut fish fillet into tikka (large cubes).

First Marination

Rub fish tikka with lemon juice, ½ of ginger garlic paste, salt, ½ of yellow chilli powder, ½ of ajwain and ½ of turmeric. Keep it for 30 minutes.

Second Marination

1. In a bowl whisk hung curd, add ginger garlic paste, salt, garam masala, yellow chilli powder, and roasted chana powder. Mix well.

2. Heat mustard oil in a pan and remove it from fire. Add remaining ajwain, turmeric and immediately add this to the above mixture. Mix well.

3. Put marinated fish pieces after removing excess moisture, into this mixture. Rub well and keep aside for 2 hours.

Cooking

1. Take a skewer and skew the marinated fish pieces one by one an inch apart, coating with remaining marinade.

2. Roast in a moderately hot tandoor or over a charcoal grill for 6-8 minutes.

3. Remove and hang the skewer to allow excess moisture to drain out completely off (3-5 minutes).

4. Baste with melted butter and roast again for 2-3 minutes.

5. Transfer to a plate and serve hot with choice of salad and chutney.

TO SERVE: 4

COOKING TIME: 8-10 Minutes

SARSON WALI MACHHLI

▼

Ingredients

Fish fillet (sole, rahu
or singhara)   -   1 kg

First Marination

Mustard paste	-	½ tsp
Ginger garlic paste	-	50 gm
Salt	-	to taste
Yellow chilli powder	-	½ tsp
Lemon juice	-	40 ml
Mustard oil	-	10 ml

Second Marination

Hung curd	-	300 ml
Ginger garlic paste	-	1 tsp
Mustard powder	-	1 tbsp
Salt	-	to taste
Yellow chilly powder	-	1 tbsp
Lemon juice	-	10 ml
Mustard oil	-	45 ml
Crushed mustard seeds	-	1 tsp
Melted butter	-	for basting

TO SERVE: 4

COOKING TIME: 8-10 Minutes

Method

Clean, cut large cubes of fish (1½" x 1½"). Wash, pat dry and keep aside.

First Marination

In a bowl mix mustard paste, ginger garlic paste, salt, yellow chilli powder, lemon juice and mustard oil. Apply this mixture to fish cubes, rub well and keep for ½ hour.

Second Marination

1. In a bowl whisk hung curd, add all the remaining ingredients in the listed order except crushed mustard seed and mustard oil. Mix and keep aside.

2. In a pan heat mustard oil, put crushed mustard seeds, saute and immediately pour it over the second marinade. Cover with a lid for a while.

3. Squeeze excess moisture from the fish and put cubes into the second marinade. Rub well and keep to marinate for 1-2 hours.

Cooking

1. Take a skewer and skew marinated fish pieces one by one an inch apart. Apply remaining marinade on fish.

2. Roast in a tandoor or over a charcoal grill at a moderate temperature for 6-8 minutes.

3. Remove and hang skewer so that the excess moisture can drain out completely (2-3 minutes).

4. Baste with melted butter. Further roast for 2-4 minutes.

5. Serve hot with choice of salad and chutney.

JUGAL BANDI SEEKH KEBAB

▼

Ingredients

Fish (sole)	-	500 gm
Prawns	-	500 gm
Ginger garlic paste	-	½ tbsp
Salt	-	to taste
White pepper powder	-	½ tbsp
Coriander (chopped)	-	20 gm
Green chilli (chopped)	-	3 nos.
Cream	-	20 ml
Melted butter	-	for basting

Method

1. Clean the fish and make a fine mince.
2. Deshell, devein and chop the prawns. Mix with the fish mince.

Marination

1. In a bowl take ginger garlic paste, salt, white pepper powder, chopped coriander, chopped green chilli, the fish mince and the chopped prawns. Rub them with your palm so that it mixes properly.
2. Add cream and mix it.
3. Divide the mixture into 16 equal portions.

Cooking

1. Spread this mixture individually on the skewer using a wet hand by pressing each portion along the length of the skewer in a cylindrical shape, one inch apart and making each kebab 4 inches long. Spread evenly.
2. Roast in a moderately hot tandoor or over a charcoal grill for 4-6 minutes.
3. Remove of hang slawer to let the excess moisture drain out completely.
3. Baste with clarified butter and further roast for 1-2 minutes.
4. Serve hot along with choice of salad and chutney.

TO SERVE: 4

COOKING TIME: 6-8 Minutes

MAHI GULMARG

▼

Ingredients

Fish fillet (sole, rahu or singhara)	-	1 kg
Hung curd	-	300 ml
Cream	-	50 ml
Garlic paste	-	30 gm
Egg	-	1 no.
Mustard paste	-	30 gm
Salt	-	To taste
Red chilli powder	-	2 tbsp
Garam masala	-	1 tbsp
Saffron	-	a pinch
Cornflour	-	60 gm
Lemon juice	-	25 ml
Refined oil	-	45 ml
Melted butter	-	for basting

Method

Clean, cut large cubes of fish (1½" x 1½"). Wash and pat dry.

Marination

In a bowl whisk hung curd. Add the remaining ingredients in the order listed. Rub well and put fish cubes into this marinade and leave it for 1-2 hours.

Cooking

1. Take a skewer and skew marinated fish pieces one by one an inch apart. Apply remaining marinade on fish.

2. Roast in a tandoor or over a charcoal grill at a moderate temperature for 6-8 minutes.

3. Remove and hang skewer so that the excess moisture can drain out completely (2-3 minutes).

4. Baste with melted butter. Further roast for 2-4 minutes.

5. Serve hot with choice of salad and chutney.

TO SERVE: 4

COOKING TIME: 8-10 Minutes

TANDOORI MACHHLI MASALA

▼

Ingredients

Fish fillet (sol, rahu or singhara)	-	I kg
Hung curd	-	300 ml
Cream	-	20 ml
Ginger garlic paste	-	15 gm
Salt	-	to taste
Garam masala powder	-	I tbsp
Crushed peppercorn	-	I tsp
Ajwain	-	I tsp
Turmeric powder	-	I tsp
Yellow chilli powder	-	2 tsp
Roasted Bengal gram flour	-	50 gm
Lemon juice	-	25 ml
Mustard oil	-	45 ml
Melted butter	-	for basting

Method

Clean and cut large cubes of fish (1½" x 1½"). Wash and pat dry.

Marination

1. In a bowl whisk hung curd, add the remaining ingredients in the order listed and mix them.

2. Put fish cubes into this marinade. Rub well and keep for 1-2 hours.

Cooking

1. Take a skewer and skew marinated fish pieces one by one an inch apart. Apply remaining marinade on fish.

3. Roast in a tandoor or over a charcoal grill at a moderate temperature for 5-6 minutes.

4. Remove and hang skewer so that the excess moisture can drain out completely (2-3 minutes).

5. Baste with melted butter. Further roast for 2-4 minutes.

6. Serve hot with choice of salad and chutney.

TO SERVE: 4

COOKING TIME: 8-10 Minutes

HARYALI MAHI TIKKA

▼

Ingredients

Fish fillet (sole, rahu or singhara)	-	I kg
Green chilli	-	20 gm
Coriander leaves	-	100 gm
Mint leaves	-	20 gm
Curry leaves	-	5 gm
Anardana	-	25 gm
Onion	-	I no.
Hung curd	-	300 gm
Ginger garlic paste	-	15 gm
Peanut paste	-	60 gm
Salt	-	to taste
Dalchini powder	-	I tsp
Kebab chini powder	-	a pinch
Crushed black pepper	-	I tsp
Crushed anardana	-	I tbsp
Ajwain powder	-	I tsp
Ginger (chopped)	-	15 gm
Cornflour	-	15 gm
Roasted gram flour	-	10 gm
Lemon juice	-	20 ml
Refined oil	-	45 ml
Melted butter	-	for basting

Method

1. Clean and cut large cubes of fish (1½" × 1½"). Wash, pat dry and keep aside.

2. In a processor put green chilli, coriander leaves, mint leaves, curry leaves, anardana, onion and make a fine paste. Transfer to a bowl.

Marination

In a bowl whisk hung curd, then add the green paste and the remaining ingredients in the order listed. Mix them. Put fish cubes into this marination. Rub well and leave for 1½-2 hours.

Cooking

1. Take a skewer and skew marinated fish pieces one by one an inch apart. Apply remaining marinade on fish.

2. Roast in a tandoor or over a charcoal grill at a moderate temperature for 6-8 minutes.

3. Remove and hang skewer so that the excess moisture can drain out completely (2-3 minutes).

4. Baste with melted butter. Further roast for 2-4 minutes.

5. Serve hot with choice of salad and chutney.

TO SERVE: 4

COOKING TIME: 8-10 Minutes

▼

Ingredients

Fish fillet (sole, rahu
or singhara)   -   I kg

First Marination

Ginger garlic paste	-	I tbsp
Ajwain	-	I tsp
Salt	-	to taste
White pepper powder	-	½ tbsp
Vinegar	-	10 ml
Refined oil	-	10 ml

Second Marination

Hung curd	-	300 ml
Ginger garlic paste	-	I ½ tbsp
Methi leaves (chopped)	-	100 gm
Green chilli (chopped)	-	2 tbsp
Salt	-	to taste
Yellow chilli powder	-	I tbsp
Kasoori methi powder	-	2 tbsp
White pepper powder	-	I tbsp
Ajwain	-	I tsp
Mustard oil	-	40 ml
Melted butter	-	for basting

Method

Clean and cut large cubes of fish (I½" × I½").
Wash and pat dry.

First Marination

In a bowl take ginger garlic paste, ajwain, salt, white
pepper powder, vinegar, oil and mix them well. Apply
this mixture to fish pieces. Rub well and keep for ½
hour.

Second Marination

1. In a bowl take hung curd, add the remaining
    ingredients in the order listed and mix well.

2. Squeeze excess moisture from the marinated fish
    and add it to the marinade. Mix well and keep
    for 1-2 hours.

Cooking

1. Take a skewer and skew marinated fish pieces
    one by one an inch apart. Apply remaining
    marinade on fish.

2. Roast in a tandoor or over a charcoal grill at a
    moderate temperature for 6-8 minutes.

3. Remove and hang skewer so that the excess
    moisture can drain out completely (2-3 minutes).

4. Baste with melted butter. Further roast for 2-4
    minutes.

5. Serve hot with choice of salad and chutney.

TO SERVE: 4

COOKING TIME: 8-10 Minutes

▼

AMRITSARI MACHHLI KEBAB

▼

Ingredients

Fish tikka (sole, rahu or singhara)	-	I kg
Ginger garlic paste	-	30 gm
Red chilli paste	-	40 gm
Salt	-	to taste
Ajwain	-	20 gm
Hung curd	-	300 ml
Cream	-	60 ml
Egg	-	I no.
Ajwain seed/powder	-	2 tbsp
Garam masala	-	I tsp
Lemon juice	-	25 ml
Refined oil	-	10 ml
Melted butter	-	for basting

Method

Clean and cut fish in large cubes ((1½" × 1½"). Wash and pat dry with a cloth.

First Marination

Apply ½ of ginger garlic paste, ½ of red chilli paste, salt, ajwain to the fish cubes. Rub well and keep for ½ hour.

Second Marination

1. In a bowl whisk hung curd, add the remaining ingredients in the order listed and mix.

2. Squeeze excess moisture from the fish and put it in the above marination. Keep it for 1½-2 hours.

Cooking

1. Take a skewer and skew marinated fish pieces one by one an inch apart. Apply remaining marinade on fish.

2. Roast in a tandoor or over a charcoal grill at moderate temperature for 6-8 minutes.

3. Remove and hang skewer so that the excess moisture can drain out completely (2-3 minutes).

4. Baste with melted butter. Further roast for 2-4 minutes.

5. Serve hot with choice of salad and chutney.

TO SERVE: 4

COOKING TIME: 8-10 Minutes

▼

Ingredients

Sole fish	-	1 kg
Salt	-	to taste
White pepper powder	-	½ tbsp
Lemon juice	-	15 ml
Tamarind pulp	-	100 gm
Jaggery	-	50 gm
Red chilly powder	-	1 tsp
Cumin powder	-	1 tsp
Garam masala	-	½ tsp
Hung curd	-	200 ml
Red chilli paste	-	1 tbsp
Melted butter	-	for basting

Method

1. Clean and cut large cube of fish. Wash, pat dry and keep aside.

2. Prepare tamarind sauce by heating tamarind pulp in a pan with little water. Add jaggery, salt, red chilli powder, cumin powder and garam masala, reduce it and cool.

First Marination

Apply salt, white pepper powder and lemon juice to the fish cubes. Keep aside for ½ hour.

Second Marination

1. In a bowl whisk hung curd and add red chilli paste, tamarind sauce and lemon juice, then mix them.

2. Remove excess moisture from the fish cubes by lightly squeezing them with your palm and dip in the above marinade. Keep aside for 1 hour.

Cooking

1. Take a skewer and skew marinated fish pieces one by one an inch apart. Apply remaining marinade on fish.

2. Roast it in a tandoor or over a charcoal grill at a moderate temperature for 6-8 minutes.

3. Remove and hang skewer so that the excess moisture can drain out completely (2-3 minutes).

4. Baste with melted butter and further roast for 2-4 minutes.

5. Serve hot with choice of salad and chutney.

TO SERVE: 4

COOKING TIME: 8-10 Minutes

▼

GULABI MAHI TIKKA

▼

Ingredients

Salmon fish fillet	-	1 kg
Salt	-	to taste
Ajwain	-	½ tbsp
White pepper powder	-	½ tbsp
Ginger garlic paste	-	2 tbsp
Processed cheese	-	150 gm
Egg white	-	1 no.
Cream	-	300 ml
Green chilli (chopped)	-	30 gm
Cornflour	-	30 gm
Melted butter	-	for basting

Method

Trim and cut large cubes of fish. Wash, pat dry and keep aside.

First Marination

Apply salt, ajwain white pepper powder and ginger garlic paste. Keep for 10-15 minutes.

Second Marination

1. In a pan, grate cheese and rub it with your palm. Add egg white, mix it, then add cream gradually so that it gets blended easily.

2. Add ginger garlic paste, salt white pepper powder, ajwain, chopped green chilli, and cornflour. Mix well.

3. Marinate fish in above marinade, rub well and keep for 10 minutes.

Cooking

1. Take a skewer and skew marinated fish pieces one by one an inch apart. Apply remaining marinade on fish.

2. Roast in a tandoor or over a charcoal grill at a moderate temperature for 3-4 minutes.

3. Remove and hang skewer so that the excess moisture drain out completely (2-3 minutes).

4. Baste with melted butter and further roast for 1-2 minutes.

5. Serve hot along with choice of salad and chutney.

TO SERVE: 4

COOKING TIME: 4-6 Minutes

Vegetarian Kebabs

▼

In the history of kebabs one finds that vegetarian kebabs were non-existent, with the exception of a few fried ones. Over the years vegetarian kebabs or vegetarian barbecue have achieved considerable significance. A large variety of vegetarian kebabs are listed in this book. These recipes are absolutely new, well tried and innovative.

One must keep in mind that vegetables when cooked in a tandoor, unlike meat retain most of their food value as the juices are sealed within by high temperature and limited cooking time.

Vegetables ideally recommended for barbecue are:

Gobhi	:	Whole baby cauliflower
Aloo	:	Whole medium-sized potato
Pyaz	:	Whole medium-sized onion
Shimla Mirch	:	Whole medium-sized capsicum
Karela	:	Whole medium-sized bitter gourd
Tamater	:	Whole large tomato
Tandoori Khumb	:	Whole fresh button mushroom
Kacha Kela	:	Raw banana
Arbi	:	Yam
Kathal	:	Jackfruit
Lauki	:	White pumpkin
Bhutta	:	Baby corn
Nadru	:	Lotus stem

TANDOORI BHARWAN PANEER

▼

Ingredients

Cottage cheese	-	500 gm
Refined oil	-	I tbsp
Cumin seed	-	½ tbsp
Turmeric	-	½ tbsp
Cabbage (chopped)	-	200 gm
Carrot (chopped)	-	50 gm
Capsicum (chopped)	-	50 gm
Salt	-	to taste
Chaat masala	-	I tsp
Coriander (chopped)	-	25 gm
Refined oil	-	for frying

Marination

Hung curd	-	400 ml
Ginger garlic paste	-	I tbsp
Red chilli paste	-	I tbsp
Salt	-	to taste
Garam masala	-	I tsp
Kasoori methi powder	-	I tsp
Lemon juice	-	I tsp
Refined oil	-	15 ml
Melted butter	-	for basting

TO SERVE: 4

COOKING TIME: 5-7 Minutes

Method

1. Trim cottage cheese block to size 5"×2½". Cut ½" thick equal slices and pat dry.

2. Heat oil in a deep pan and fry these slices till golden brown and keep aside.

Stuffing

1. Heat oil in a pan, add cumin seeds and sauté till it starts crackling. Add turmeric and all the vegetables. Sauté for 2-3 minutes.

2. Add salt, chaat masala, chopped coriander and cook till vegetables are crisp. Remove from fire and cool.

3. Place fine slices of cottage cheese on a flat surface or tray. Spread the cooked vegetable mixture in equal portions individually. Spread the mixture using a knife and roll each slice into a cylindrical shape and prick it with toothpick from both ends so that it holds the stuffing. Keep aside.

Marination

1. Put hung curd in a bowl. Add ginger garlic paste, red chilli paste, salt, garam masala, kasoori methi powder, lemon juice, refined oil and mix well.

2. Put stuffed cottage cheese roll in the above marinade and keep it for I hour.

Cooking

1. Take a skewer and skew marinated paneer roll, leaving a one inch gap in between.

2. Roast in a tandoor or over a charcoal grill at a moderate temperature for 5-7 minutes.

3. Cut each roll in 2-3 slices.

4. Baste with melted butter whole cooking.

5. Serve hot along with a choice of salad and chutney.

TANDOORI PANEER PATAKA

▼

Ingredients

Cottage cheese	-	850 gm

Stuffing

Mint chutney	-	100 gm
Grated paneer	-	50 gm
Salt	-	to taste

Marination

Processed cheese	-	100 gm
Egg white	-	1 no.
Cream	-	200 ml
Cashewnut paste	-	50 gm
Ginger garlic paste	-	½ tbsp
Salt	-	to taste
White pepper powder	-	½ tsp
Elaichi javitri powder	-	a little
Melted butter	-	for basting

Method

Cut cottage cheese in large equal cubes. Slit the cottage cheese in the centre without disjoining for stuffing. Pat dry and keep aside.

Stuffing

In a bowl put mint chutney, grated paneer and salt. Stuff this green paste inside each paneer cube in equal quantity and keep aside.

Marination

1. In a tray grate cheese, egg white and mash it with your palm until the cheese blends well.

2. Add cream gradually so that it gets blended in the mixture. Mix to a smooth consistency.

3. Add cashewnut paste, ginger garlic paste, salt, white pepper powder and elaichi javitri powder.

4. Put stuffed cottage cheese into this mixture and leave it to marinate for 2-3 hours.

Cooking

1. Take a skewer and skew marinated cottage cheese cubes leaving a gap of one inch between each.

2. Roast in a tandoor or over a charcoal grill at a moderate temperature for 6-8 minutes.

3. Paste with melted butter whole cooking.

4. Serve hot along with choice of salad and chutney.

TO SERVE: 4

COOKING TIME: 6-8 Minutes

▼

Ingredients
Cottage cheese   -   950 gm

Stuffing
Garlic paste	-	45 gm
Salt	-	to taste
Garam masala	-	1 tsp
Red chilli powder	-	1½ tbsp
Tandoori masala	-	1 tbsp
Anardana (crushed)	-	2 tbsp
Vinegar	-	3 tsp
Mustard oil	-	60 ml

First Marination
Hung curd	-	100 ml
Cream	-	25 ml
Ginger garlic paste	-	15 gm
Egg (optional)	-	1 no.
Salt	-	to taste
Garam masala	-	1 tsp
Red chilli powder	-	1 tbsp
Turmeric	-	1 tsp
Roasted gram flour	-	2 tbsp
Lemon juice	-	10 ml
Refined oil	-	20 ml

Second Marination
Hung curd	-	100 ml
Cream	-	25 ml
Ginger garlic paste	-	15 gm
Green paste	-	4 tbsp
Egg (optional)	-	1 no.
Salt	-	to taste
White pepper powder	-	1 tsp
Ajwain	-	1 tsp
Gram flour (roasted)	-	2 tbsp
Lemon juice	-	10 ml
Refined oil	-	20 ml
Melted butter	-	for basting

TO SERVE: 4

COOKING TIME: 6-8 Minutes

DORANGA PANEER TIKKA

▼

Method

1. Cut paneer into 2½" thick slices. Further slice each piece half way without disjoining it. In total make 24 pieces.

2. In a bowl take garlic paste, salt, garam masala, red chilli powder, tandoori masala, crushed anardana, vinegar, mustard oil and mix thoroughly.

3. Stuff this mixture in each slice of paneer with the help of a knife. Press and keep aside.

First Marination

In a bowl take hung curd, add cream, ginger garlic paste, salt, green paste, egg, garam masala, lemon juice, red chilli powder, turmeric, roasted gram flour, refined oil and mix well. Put half of the stuffed paneer slice into this batter and keep aside for 1 hour.

Second Marination

In a bowl take hung curd, add cream, ginger garlic paste, egg, salt, white pepper powder, ajwain, roasted gram flour, lemon juice, refined oil and mix well. Put remaining stuffed paneer slice in this batter and keep it for 1 hour.

Cooking

1. Take a skewer and skew marinated paneer pieces alternately with both the marinations leaving a gap of one inch between each portion.

2. Roast it in a tandoor or over a charcoal grill at a moderate temperature for 6-8 minutes.

3. Baste with melted butter whole cooking.

4. Serve hot along with choice of salad and chutney.

PANEER TIKKA KALIMIRCH

▼

Ingredients

Cottage cheese	-	950 gm
Boiled onion paste	-	50 gm
Cream	-	50 ml
Ginger garlic paste	-	15 gm
Egg (optional)	-	1 no.
Salt	-	to taste
Black pepper (crushed)	-	3 tbsp
Lemon rind	-	2 nos.
Refined flour (roasted)	-	50 gm
Cornflour	-	50 gm
Refined oil	-	40 ml

Method

Cut cottage cheese into large cubes (size 1½"×1½"). Pat dry and keep aside. Give a slit in the centre without disjoining.

Marination

1. In a bowl put boiled onion paste, cream, ginger garlic paste, salt, crushed pepper, lemon rind, roasted refined flour, cornflour, refined oil and mix well.

2. Put cottage cheese pieces into this marinade. Also insert marinade into the paneer with the help of your finger to slit part. Keep for 2-3 hours.

Cooking

1. Take a skewer and skew marinated cottage cheese leaving a gap of one inch between portions.

2. Roast in a tandoor or over a charcoal grill at a moderate temperature for 6-8 minutes. Half onion or potato can be used to prevent slipping of cottage cheese.

3. Serve hot with choice of salad and chutney.

TO SERVE: 4

COOKING TIME: 6-8 Minutes

▼

ACHARI PANEER TIKKA

▼

Ingredients

Cottage cheese	-	850 gm
Mustard oil	-	50 ml
Mustard seed	-	½ tsp
Methi dana	-	a few
Kalonji	-	¼ tsp
Saunf (fennel seed)	-	1 tsp
Hung curd	-	300 ml
Ginger garlic paste	-	1½ tbsp
Salt	-	to taste
Yellow chilly powder	-	1 tsp
Turmeric	-	1 tsp
Achar ka masala	-	100 gm

Method

1. Cut cottage cheese in cubes (size 1½" × 1½"), pat dry and keep aside.

2. Heat the mustard oil in a pan, add methi dana, saute until it crackles. Add mustard seeds, kalonji, saunf and saute for 2-3 minutes. Remove and keep aside this mustard mixture to cool.

Marination

1. In a bowl whisk hung curd, add ginger garlic paste, mustard mixture, salt, yellow chilly powder, turmeric, achar ka masala and mix well.

2. Put paneer cubes into this mixture and keep for 2-3 hours in the refrigerator.

Cooking

1. Take a skewer and skew marinated cottage cheese cubes one by one leaving one inch gap between each.

2. Roast in a tandoor or over a charcoal grill at a moderate temperature for 6-8 minutes.

3. Serve hot along with choice of salad and chutney.

TO SERVE: 4

COOKING TIME: 6-8 Minutes

KASOORI PANEER TIKKA

▼

Ingredients

Cottage cheese	-	850 gm
Hung curd	-	300 ml
Ginger garlic paste	-	I tbsp
Salt	-	to taste
Yellow chilli powder	-	I tsp
Kasoori methi powder	-	I½ tbsp
Lemon juice	-	20 ml
Mustard oil	-	I5 ml

Method

Cut cottage cheese in large cubes (size I½"×I½"). Pat dry and keep aside.

Marination

1. In a bowl beat hung curd, add ginger garlic paste, yellow chilli powder, kasoori methi powder, salt, lemon juice, mustard oil and mix well.

2. Put paneer cubes into this marination and keep it for I-2 hours in refrigeration.

Cooking

1. Take a skewer and skew marinated cubes leaving one inch gap between each.

2. Roast in a tandoor or over a charcoal grill at a moderate temperature for 6-8 minutes.

3. Serve hot along with choice of salad and chutney.

TO SERVE: 4

COOKING TIME: 6-8 Minutes

TIRANGA PANEER TIKKA

▼

Ingredients

Cottage cheese	-	950 gm
Mint chutney	-	50 gm
Khoya	-	50 gm
Saffron	-	a pinch
Salt	-	to taste
Red chilli powder	-	½ tbsp
Hung curd	-	300 ml
Ginger garlic paste	-	1 tbsp
Coriander (chopped)	-	20 gm
Green chilly (chopped)	-	10 gm
Salt	-	to taste
White pepper powder	-	1 tbsp
Lemon juice	-	20 ml
Melted butter	-	for basting

Method

1. Cut paneer into large cubes size (1½" × 1½").

2. Cut each cube into 3 layers without disjoining.

3. In a small bowl grate khoya. Mash it and add saffron, salt and mix well. In another bowl mash paneer (100gm), red chilli powder, salt and mix well.

4. With the help of a knife stuff each slice in this order, i.e., mint chutney in the first layer, mashed paneer in the second layer and khoya paste in the third layer in equal portions. (Sprinkle a pinch of salt before stuffing.)

Marination

1. Take a bowl put hung curd, the remaining ingredients and mix well.

2. Put stuffed cottage cheese pieces in this marinade and keep for 1 hour.

Cooking

1. Take a skewer and skew marinated cottage cheese leaving a gap of one inch between each portion.

2. Roast it in a tandoor over a charcoal grill at a moderate temperature for 6-8 minutes.

3. Baste with melted butter while cooking.

4. Serve hot along with choice of salad and chutney.

TO SERVE: 4

COOKING TIME: 6-8 Minutes

TIRANGA PANEER TIKKA

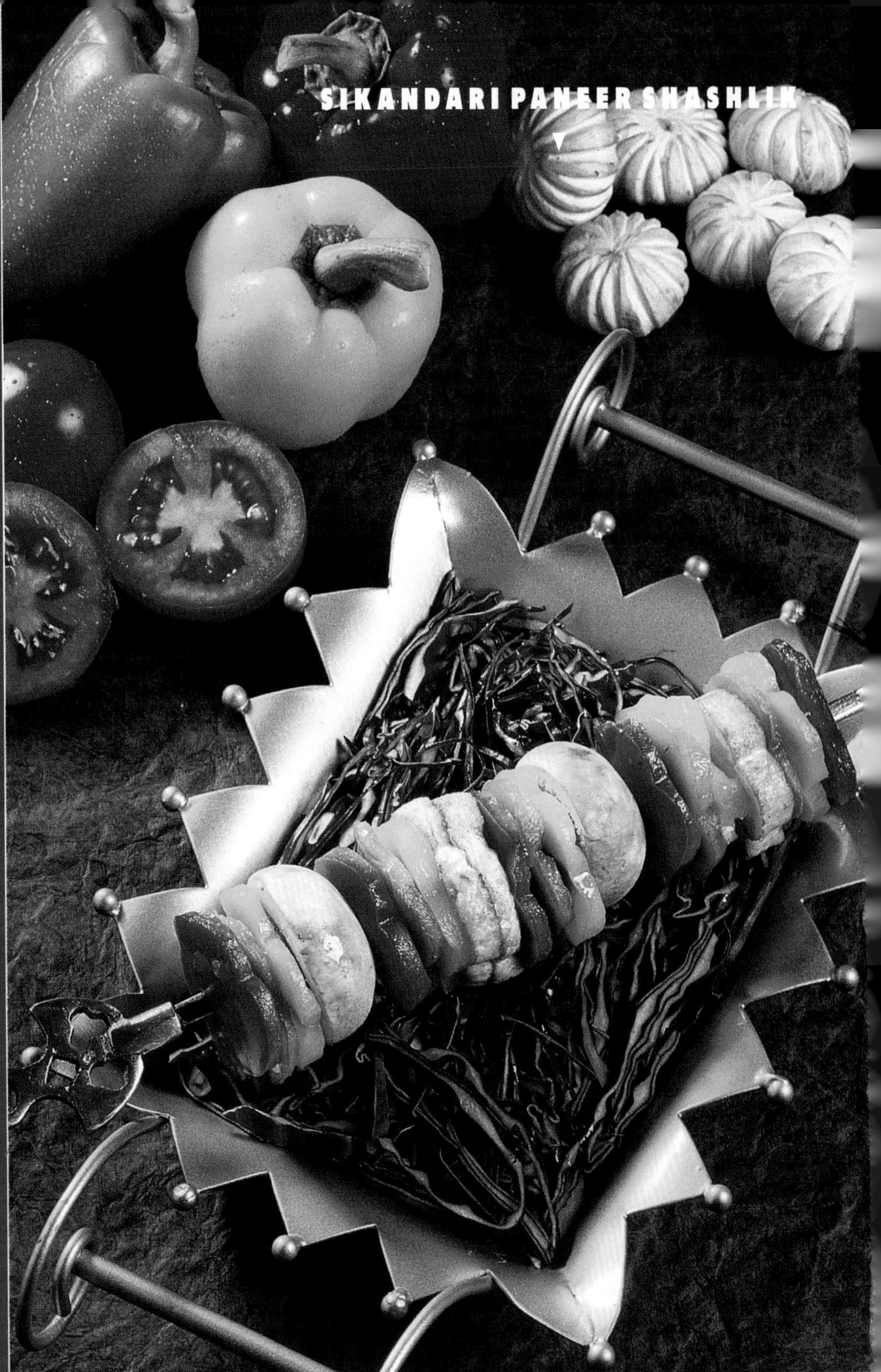
SIKANDARI PANEER SHASHLIK

SIKANDARI PANEER SHASHLIK

▼

Ingredients

Cottage cheese	-	800 gm
Tomatoes	-	100 gm
Capsicum	-	100 gm
Onion	-	100 gm
Hung curd	-	300 ml
Ginger garlic paste	-	1 tbsp
Red chilli paste	-	2 tbsp
Salt	-	to taste
Kasoori methi powder	-	1 tbsp
Garam masala	-	1 tbsp
Lemon juice	-	20 ml
Refined oil	-	40 ml
Melted butter	-	for basting

TO SERVE: 4

COOKING TIME: 6-8 Minutes

Method

1. Cut paneer into large cubes (1½×1½"). Pat dry with a cloth.

2. Cut tomato into 4 and deseed. Cut capsicum into 4 and deseed. Peel and cut onions into 4. Make large cubes of equal size and keep aside.

Marination

1. In a bowl put hung curd, add ginger garlic paste, red chilli paste, salt, kasoori methi powder, garam masala, lemon juice, oil and mix well.

2. Put paneer cubes and vegetable cubes into this marinade and keep for 1 hour.

Cooking

1. Take a skewer and skew marinated cottage cheese and vegetable alternately.

2. Roast in a tandoor or over a charcoal grill at a moderate temperature for 6-8 minutes. Baste with melted butter while cooking.

3. Serve hot along with choice of salad and chutney.

KHATTA MEETHA PANEER TIKKA

▼

Ingredients

Cottage cheese	-	850 gm
Coriander leaves	-	100 gm
Raw mango	-	50 gm
Mango chutney	-	75 gm
Curry leaves	-	4-6 nos.
Green chilli	-	25 gm
Ginger garlic paste	-	10 gm
Salt	-	to taste
Red chilli powder	-	5 gm
Chaat masala	-	5 gm
Cornflour	-	10 gm
Refined oil	-	20 ml

Method

1. Cut each paneer into thick cubes and further cut each cube from the centre without disjoining. Pat dry and keep aside.

2. In a processor put coriander leaves, raw mango, mango chutney, curry leaves, green chillies and salt. Make a fine paste. Transfer it to a bowl.

3. Stuff each paneer piece equally with this green paste by using a knife. Retain ¼ of the green paste for further marination.

Marination

1. In a bowl put the remaining green paste, add ginger garlic paste, red chilli powder, chaat masala, cornflour and refined oil.

2. Put stuffed paneer into this marination and keep aside for 1-2 hours.

Cooking

1. Take a skewer and skew marinated cottage cheese leaving a gap of an inch between each portion.

2. Roast in a tandoor or over a charcoal grill at a moderate temperature for 6-8 minutes.

3. Serve hot along with choice of salad and chutney.

TO SERVE: 4

COOKING TIME: 6-8 Minutes

LAHORI PANEER TIKKA

▼

Ingredients

Cottage cheese	-	850 gm
Hung curd	-	300 ml
Cream	-	30 ml
Garlic paste	-	15 gm
Red chilli paste	-	30 gm
Mint chutney	-	60 gm
Egg (optional)	-	1 no.
Black salt	-	to taste
Yellow chilli powder	-	2 tsp
Gram flour (roasted)	-	2 tbsp
Mustard oil	-	40 ml

Method

Cut cottage cheese into large cubes (size 1½"×1½") and pat dry with a cloth.

Marination

1. In a bowl put hung curd, add cream, garlic paste, red chilli paste, mint chutney, egg, black salt, yellow chilly powder, roasted gram flour, mustard oil and mix thoroughly.

2. Put paneer cubes into the marinade and keep for 1-2 hours in refrigeration.

Cooking

1. Take a skewer and skew marinated cottage cheese cubes one by one leaving a one inch gap between each.

2. Roast in a tandoor or over a charcoal grill at a moderate temperature for 6-8 minutes.

3. Serve hot along with choice of salad and chutney.

TO SERVE: 4

COOKING TIME: 6-8 Minutes

RESHMI PANEER SEEKH

▼

Ingredients

Cottage cheese	-	600 gm
Boiled potato	-	150 gm
Green chilli (chopped)	-	25 gm
Coriander (chopped)	-	20 gm
Capsicum (chopped)	-	50 gm
Tomatoes (chopped)	-	50 gm
Salt	-	to taste
Yellow chilli powder	-	1 tsp
Chana powder	-	2 tbsp
Melted butter	-	2 tbsp
Saffron	-	a pinch

Method

1. In a bowl grate cottage cheese and peeled boiled potatoes.

2. Add chopped green chillies, coriander, capsicum, tomatoes and mix well.

3. Add salt, yellow chilli powder, channa powder, melted butter. Sprinkle saffron in the end and mix to form a smooth dough.

4. Divide the mixture into 16 equal portions and make balls.

Cooking

1. Take a skewer and apply the mixture along the skewer with moist hands, in a cylindrical shape. Roast in a moderate tandoor or over a charcoal grill for 6-8 minutes.

2. Serve hot along with choice of salad and chutney.

TO SERVE: 4

COOKING TIME: 6-8 Minutes

TANDOORI HARI GOBHI

▼

Ingredients

Broccoli	-	4 nos.
Salt	-	to taste
Peppercorn	-	6 nos.
Dalchini	-	2 nos.
Big cardamom	-	4 nos.
Cloves	-	4 nos.
Hung curd	-	350 ml
Ginger garlic paste	-	I tbsp
Yellow chilli powder	-	I½ tbsp
Garam masala	-	45 ml
Turmeric	-	I tbsp

Method

1. Clean and cut brocolli into medium-size flowerettes.

2. Heat water in a vessel add salt, peppercorn, dalchinni, big cardamom, cloves and blanch broccoli in it till 2/3rd cooked. Drain and cool it.

Marination

1. In a bowl take hung curd, add ginger garlic paste salt, yellow chilli powder, garam masala, and mix well.

2. Heat mustard oil in a pan, add turmeric to it. Pour this in curd mixture and mix well.

3. Put blanched brocob in this mixture and keep to marinate for I hour.

Cooking

1. Take a skewer, skew marinated broccolli pieces, put remaining marinade on top and roast in a tandoor or over a charcoal grill for 6-8 minutes.

2. Serve hot with choice of salad and chutney.

TO SERVE: 4

COOKING TIME: 6-8 Minutes

▼

NOORANI KEBAB

Ingredients

Cottage cheese	-	500 gm
Boiled potato	-	300 gm
Garlic paste	-	30 gm
Egg yolk (optional)	-	1 no.
Onion (chopped)	-	30 gm
Curry leaves (chopped)	-	15 gm
Garlic (chopped)	-	50 gm
Coriander (chopped)	-	30 gm
Salt	-	to taste
White pepper powder	-	1 tbsp
Elaichi javitri powder	-	a pinch
Tandoori masala	-	½ tbsp
Maida	-	2 tbsp
Bread crumbs	-	for binding

Method

1. In a bowl grate cottage cheese and peeled boiled potatoes, add garlic paste and egg yolk.

2. Add chopped onion, curry leaves, garlic, coriander, salt, white pepper powder, elaichi javitri powder, tandoori masala, maida and bread crumbs. Mix them and make a smooth dough. Divide this mixture into 16 equal portions and make balls.

Cooking

1. Take a skewer. Apply each ball on it with moist hands in a cylindrical shape and grill over charcoal or in a tandoor at a moderate temperature for 6-8 minutes.

2. Serve hot with choice of salad and chutney.

TO SERVE: 4

COOKING TIME: 6-8 Minutes

LAHSUNI PANEER TIKKA

▼

Ingredients

Cottage cheese	-	850 gm
Hung curd	-	300 gm
Cream	-	50 ml
Garlic paste	-	30 gm
Egg (optional)	-	1 no.
Garlic (chopped)	-	10 gm
Green chilli (chopped)	-	5 gm
Coriander (chopped)	-	45gm
Salt	-	to taste
Red chilli powder	-	1½ tbsp
Turmeric powder	-	½ tbsp
Garam masala	-	1½ tbsp
Ajwain powder	-	1 tbsp
Chaat masala	-	1 tbsp
Gram flour (roasted)	-	4 tbsp
Refined oil	-	30 ml

Stuffing

Garlic paste	-	60 gm
Tandoori masala	-	2 tbsp

Method

1. Cut cottage cheese into square cubes (1½" × 1½"). Give a slit from the centre without disjoining. Keep aside.

2. In a bowl put garlic paste, tandoori masala and mix. Apply this mixture equally inside the cottage cheese with your finger. Keep aside.

Marination

1. Take hung curd in a bowl add cream, garlic paste, egg, chopped garlic, green chilli, coriander, salt, red chilli powder, turmeric, garam masala, ajwain powder, chaat masala, roasted gram flour, vinegar, refined oil and mix thoroughly.

2. Put stuffed paneer pieces into this marinade and keep aside for 1½-2 hours.

Cooking

1. Take a skewer and skew paneer pieces one by one keeping a one inch gap in between each (half cut onion or small potato can be used to prevent slipping).

2. Roast/ grill over charcoal or in a tandoor at a moderate temperature for 6-8 minutes

3. Serve hot with choice of salad and chutney.

TO SERVE: 4

COOKING TIME: 6-8 Minutes

HARE MATAR KE SHAMMI KEBAB

▼

Ingredients .

Green peas	-	600 gm
Boiled potatoes	-	100 gm
Cottage cheese	-	100 gm
Green chilli (chopped)	-	2 nos
Ginger (chopped)	-	15 gm
Coriander (chopped)	-	25 gm
Ginger garlic paste	-	1 tsp
Black salt	-	to taste
Yellow chilli powder	-	1 tsp
Garam masala	-	1 tsp
Chana powder	-	50 gm
Refined oil	-	for frying

Method

1. Wash and boil green peas until tender and drain. Squeeze water by using a cloth. Transfer to a bowl and mash them by using a ladle or wooden spoon.

2. Grate boiled potatoes and cottage cheese. Add this to green peas along with chopped green chilli, ginger, coriander, garam masala, chana powder and mix thoroughly.

3. Add ginger garlic paste, black salt, yellow chilly powder and mix well until it forms into a smooth dough.

4. Divide this mixture into 16 equal portions. Make balls and press between your palm to shape them round like a medallion (tikki).

Cooking

1. Heat oil in a pan and deep fry kebabs until crisp and golden brown.

2. Serve hot with choice of salad and chutney.

TO SERVE: 4

COOKING TIME: 2-3 Minutes

SUBZ GALOUTI KEBAB

▼

Ingredients

Beans	-	600 gm
Carrots	-	250 gm
Baby corn	-	50 gm
Cauliflower	-	150 gm
Grean peas	-	100 gm
Mushroom	-	50 gm
Ginger garlic paste	-	½ tbsp
Salt	-	to taste
Yellow chilly powder	-	1½ tsp
Garam masala	-	½ tsp
Elaich javitri powder	-	a pinch
Boiled potato	-	100 gm
Cloves	-	4-6 nos
Oil	-	for frying
Ghee	-	1 tbsp

TO SERVE: 4

COOKING TIME: 3-4 Minutes

Method

1. String beans, peel carrots, cut cauliflower and baby corn into small pieces and wash. Cook these vegetables in boiling water until tender. Drain and squeeze water by using a cloth.

2. Similarly parboil green peas and mushroom. Drain and squeeze water.

3. In a processor put all the boiled vegetables and make a fine mince. Transfer it to a bowl. Add ginger garlic paste, yellow chilli powder, salt, garam masala, elaichi javitri powder and mix thoroughly.

4. In a bowl grate boiled potatoes then add boiled vegetable mixture and mix well.

5. Put this mixture in a large pot. In a small bowl put pieces of burning charcoal and place beside the vegetable mixture. Put cloves and pour ghee and cover the pot with a lid for 3-5 minutes so that it gets a smoking flavour.

6. Open the lid, remove the mixture.

Cooking

1. Divide the mixture into 16 equal portions. Make small balls and press between your palm to give a round shape like a medallion (tikki).

2. Heat oil in a non-stick pan and shallow fry until golden brown from both sides.

3. Serve hot with choice of salad and chutney.

TANDOORI PYAZ

▼

Ingredients

Onion (medium)   -   8 nos.

Stuffing

Mustard oil	-	25 ml
Fennel seeds	-	a few
Mustard seeds	-	a few
Kalonji seeds	-	a few
Onion (chopped)	-	150 gm
Salt	-	to taste
Achari masala	-	75 gm
Gram flour	-	100 gm
Cornflour	-	30 gm
Salt	-	to taste
Lemon juice	-	15 ml
Coriander (chopped)	-	20 gm
Ginger garlic paste	-	1 tbsp
Red chilly paste	-	1 tbsp
Hung curd	-	200 ml
Kasoori methi powder	-	1 tsp
Garam masala	-	1 tsp

Method

1. Peel and wash onion. Squeeze water by using a dry cloth.

2. With a sharp knife or the tip of a peeler, scoop the onion ½ inch deep and keep aside.

Stuffing

1. Heat mustard oil in a pan, add fennel seeds, mustard seeds and kalonji seeds and allow it to crackle. Add chopped onions and fry until golden brown. Add achari masala, salt and transfer it to a bowl and let it cool.

2. Stuff each onion with cooked masala and keep aside.

Marination

1. Prepare thick marinade with gram flour, cornflour, salt, lemon juice, chopped coriander, ginger garlic paste, red chilli paste, kasoori methi powder, garam masala and hung curd. Mix well to a smooth paste.

2. Dip stuffed onions into this batter and leave to rest for 30 minutes.

Cooking

1. Take a skewer and skew the marinated onions one by one keeping a one-inch gap between each.

2. Roast over a charcoal grill or in a tandoor at a moderate temperature till the batter becomes brown and crispy (6-8 minutes).

3. Cut the onions into four and serve hot with choice of salad and chutney.

TO SERVE: 4

COOKING TIME: 6-8 Minutes

TANDOORI SUBZ SHASHLIK

▼

Ingredients

Pineapple	-	200 gm
Capsicum	-	200 gm
Tomato	-	200 gm
Onion	-	200 gm
Salt	-	to taste
Red chilli powder	-	2 tbsp
Kasoori methi powder	-	1 tbsp
Garam masala	-	2 tbsp
Vinegar	-	100 ml
Refined oil	-	200 ml

Method

1. Cut pineapple into large cubes (1½" × 1½"). Deseed capsicum, tomato and cut in large cubes. Peel and cut onions in cubes and keep aside.

2. In a bowl take salt, red chilli powder, kasoori methi powder, garam masala, vinegar, refined oil. Add diced vegetable and mix thoroughly. Keep aside for 1 hour.

Cooking

1. Take a skewer and skew pineapple, capsicum, onion, tomato alternately. Put remaining marinade on top.

2. Roast in a tandoor or over a charcoal grill at a moderate temperature for 6-8 minutes.

3. Serve hot with choice of salad and chutney.

TO SERVE: 4

COOKING TIME: 6-8 Minutes

▼

BHARWAN PHOOL GOBHI

▼

Ingredients

Cauliflower (medium)	-	4 nos.
Pepper corn	-	5 nos.
Cardamom (big)	-	3 nos.
Cardamom (small)	-	5 nos.
Dalchini	-	2 nos.
Cloves	-	5 nos.

Stuffing

Oil	-	50 ml
Ground urad dal	-	10 gm
Cashewnut (chopped)	-	15 gm
Almond slices	-	15 gm
Green chilli (chopped)	-	10 gm
Coriander (chopped)	-	20 gm
Khoya (grated)	-	25 gm
Salt	-	to taste

First Marination

Ginger garlic paste	-	1 tbsp
Mustard paste	-	1 tsp
Oil	-	10 ml
Turmeric powder	-	1 tsp
Salt	-	to taste

Second Marination

Lemon juice	-	15 ml
Grated cheese	-	50 gm
Cream	-	100 ml
Curd	-	50 ml
Green chilly (chopped)	-	10 gm
Coriander (chopped)	-	20 gm
Salt	-	to taste
White pepper powder	-	1 tbsp

TO SERVE: 4

COOKING TIME: 8-10 Minutes

Method

1. Remove stem without disjoining the cauliflower.

2. Parboil cauliflower with pepper corn, cardamom (big), cardamom, dalchini and cloves. Drain water and let it cool.

Stuffing

1. Heat oil in a pan, put ground urad dal and fry until oil is separated. Transfer it to a bowl, add chopped cashewnuts, almond slices, chopped green chillies, coriander, salt and khoya. Mix well.

2. Stuff this mixture inside cauliflower in between the florets and keep aside.

First Marination

In a bowl put ginger garlic paste, mustard paste, turmeric powder salt, oil and mix well. Apply arinade all around and keep aside for 1 hour.

Second Marination

In a bowl combine all the remaining ingredients and mix well. Apply this marinade to the cauliflower and leave for 1 hour.

Cooking

1. Take a skewer and skew cauliflower leaving a gap of 1 inch between each portion.

2. Roast in a tandoor at a moderate temperature for 8-10 minutes.

3. Serve hot with choice of salad and chutney.

TANDOORI ACHARI KHUMB

▼

Ingredients

Large fresh mushrooms	-	32 pieces
Hung curd	-	200 ml
Achari paste	-	100 gm
Ginger garlic paste	-	15 gm
Mustard powder	-	½ tsp
Kalonji	-	2 tsp
Gram flour (roasted)	-	3 tbsp
Mustard oil	-	150 ml
Egg (optional)	-	1 no.
Salt	-	to taste
Turmeric	-	1 tsp
Garam masala	-	2 tsp
Red chilli paste	-	2 tsp

Method

1. Remove stems and wash mushroom in running water.

2. Parboil mushrooms. Drain and immediately put in cold water. Again drain and squeeze excess water from the mushrooms.

Marination

1. In a bowl take hung curd, add achari paste, ginger garlic paste, mustard powder, kalonji, roasted gram flour, mustard oil, egg, salt, turmeric powder garam masala, red chilli paste and mix well.

2. Put blanched mushrooms in the marinade and keep aside for 1-2 hours.

Cooking

1. Take a skewer and skew marinated mushrooms one by one, apple remaining marinade only.

2. Roast in a tandoor at a moderate temperature or over a charcoal grill for 4-6 minutes.

3. Serve hot with choice of salad and chutney.

TO SERVE: 4

COOKING TIME: 4-6 Minutes

▼

Ingredients

Potato (medium size)	-	8 nos.

Marination

Hung curd	-	300 ml
Cream	-	100 ml
Ginger garlic paste	-	15 gm
Red chilli paste	-	30 gm
Salt	-	to taste
Ajwain powder	-	¼ tsp
Garam masala	-	1 tsp
Gram flour (roasted)	-	60 gm
Lemon juice	-	30 gm
Refined oil	-	100 ml

Stuffing

Fried potato trimming	-	150 gm
Cottage cheese	-	150 gm
Onion (chopped)	-	30 gm
Ginger (chopped)	-	15 gm
Green chilli (chopped)	-	10 gm
Coriander (chopped)	-	15 gm
Salt	-	to taste
Yellow chilli powder	-	½ tsp
Elaichi javitri powder	-	a pinch
Chaat masala	-	2 tsp
Shahi jeera	-	1 tsp
Grated cheese	-	100 gm
Clarified butter	-	30 ml

TO SERVE: 4

COOKING TIME: 4-5 Minutes

Method

1. Peel potatoes, cut off the circle from the longer end. With a sharp knife gently scoop out the flesh within (1 inch deep). Wash and pat dry with a cloth. Keep potato flesh aside.

2. Heat oil in a pan and deep fry scooped potatoes until half cooked. Also fry potato flesh until cooked and put it in a bowl and mash it.

Stuffing

In a bowl put cottage cheese and mash it with a wooden spoon/hand. Add mashed potatoes, chopped ginger, coriander, green chilli, onion, salt, yellow chilli powder, elaichi javitri powder, chaat masala, shahi jeera, grated cheese and mix well. Stuff this mixture into fried scooped potatoes and keep aside.

Marination

1. In a bowl take hung curd, add cream, ginger garlic paste, red chilli paste, salt, ajwain powder, garam masala, roasted gram flour, lemon juice, refined oil and mix well.

2. Put stuffed potatoes into this marinade. Dip them properly and keep for 1 hour.

Cooking

1. Take a skewer and skew marinated potatoes one by one an inch apart and roast in a tandoor at a moderate temperature until the batter becomes golden brown and crispy.

2. Serve hot with choice of salad and chutney.

▼

TANDOORI BHARWAN TAMATAR

▼

Ingredients

Tomato (large)	-	8 nos.

Stuffing

Oil	-	10 ml
Cumin seeds	-	1 tsp
Paneer cubes (small)	-	300 gm
Boiled potatoes (small)	-	300 gm
Green peas	-	150 gm
Raisins	-	25 gm
Salt	-	to taste
Turmeric powder	-	½ tsp
Red chilli powder	-	1 tsp

Marination

Egg	-	2 nos
Gram flour	-	100 gm
Salt	-	to taste
Ajwain	-	a pinch
Hung curd	-	100 gm

Method

Cut caps of the tomatoes, remove seeds, wash and pat dry with a cloth.

Stuffing

1. Heat oil in a non-stick pan, add cumin seeds. Let it crackle, add paneer cubes and diced potato, green peas and raisins, salt, turmeric powder, and red chilli powder. Saute for 1-2 minutes and transfer this mixture in a bowl and allow to cool.

2. Stuff each tomato with this mixture. Cover with the caps and individually tie each tomato with a kitchen string.

Marination

Prepare marination by adding egg, gram flour, salt, ajwain, hung curd and mix thoroughly.

Cooking

1. Coat the tomatoes with the batter. Take a skewer and skew the tomatoes leaving at least a one-inch gap. Half cut onion or potato can be used to avoid slipping of tomatoes.

2. Roast over a charcoal grill or in a moderately hot tandoor for 3-5 minutes.

3. Serve hot with choice of salad and chutney.

TO SERVE: 4

COOKING TIME: 3-5 Minutes

▼

Ingredients

Potato (large)	-	8 nos.

Stuffing

Cornflour	-	for coating
Sesame seeds	-	for coating
Refined oil	-	for frying
Oil/butter	-	20 ml
Cumin seeds	-	I tsp
Turmeric powder	-	I tsp
Cottage cheese (diced)	-	200 gm
Boiled potato (diced)	-	150 gm
Green peas	-	100 gm
Raisins (chopped)	-	20 gm
Salt	-	to taste
Red chilly powder	-	I tsp
Coriander (chopped)	-	20 gm

Method

1. Peel potatoes, cut the tip from one side with a sharp knife and make a hollow at least I inch deep. Wash and pat dry with a cloth.

2. Heat water in a pan and blanch these potatoes, strain and dry well.

3. Heat oil in a kadai. In the mean time put cornflour in a bowl, add water to it and mix it thoroughly to make a batter of coating consistency. Steep the blanched potatoes in it and then roll in sesame seeds. Deep fry on slow flame until half-cooked. Ensure that potatoes do not turn brown during frying. Remove and keep them on a piece of cloth (upside down) to remove excess oil.

Stuffing

1. In a non-stick pan heat oil, put cumin seeds and sauté for a few seconds. Add turmeric powder with all the remaining ingredients, sauté for 2-3 minutes, remove it on a tray and allow it to cool.

2. Divide the mixture into eight equal portions, stuff each potato with this mixture.

Cooking

1. Take a skewer and skew each potato one by one leaving a gap of I inch.
2. Roast it in a tandoor for 3-5 minutes until golden brown.
3. Remove and cut in thick slices.
4. Serve hot along with choice of salad and chutney.

TO SERVE: 4

COOKING TIME: 3-5 Minutes

▼

BHUTTA SEEKH KEBAB ▾

BHUTTA SEEKH KEBAB

▼

Ingredients

Baby corn	-	700 gm
Turmeric powder	-	I tbsp
Cottage cheese	-	250 gm
Green chilli (chopped)	-	I tbsp
Ginger garlic paste	-	I tsp
Coriander (chopped)	-	3 tbsp
Ginger (chopped)	-	I tsp
Kashmiri red chilli powder	-	I tsp
Garam masala	-	I tbsp
Chaat masala	-	I tsp
Tandoori masala	-	I tsp
Melted butter	-	I tbsp
Bread crumbs	-	for binding
Salt	-	to taste

Method

1. Clean, wash and cook baby corn in boiling water with a pinch of turmeric powder until tender. Drain water and keep aside to cool.

2. In a bowl mash cheese, add 600 gm of boiled corn to it, reserving the balance for later use.

3. Add all the ingredients and mix well with the help of your palm. Check seasoning and keep aside.

4. Divide this mixture into 16 equal portions and make balls.

Cooking

1. Take a skewer and apply mixture along on it with a moist palm. Put remaining corn on top of this mixture.

2. Roast in a moderately hot tandoor or over a charcoal grill for 8-10 minutes.

3. Serve hot with a choice of salad and chutney.

TO SERVE: 4

COOKING TIME: 8-10 Minutes

SHIMLA MIRCH NISHAT

▼

Ingredients

Capsicum (large)   -   8 nos.

Stuffing

Refined oil	-	10 ml
Cumin seeds	-	1 tsp
Paneer cubes (small)	-	300 gm
Boiled potatoes (small)	-	300 gm
Green peas	-	150 gm
Roasted cashew nut	-	20 gm
Raisins	-	25 gm
Salt	-	to taste
Turmeric powder	-	½ tsp
Red chilli powder	-	1 tsp

Method

Cut the caps of capsicum and remove the seeds, wash and keep aside.

Stuffing

1. Heat oil in a non-stick pan, add cumin seeds and let it crackle. Add paneer cubes and diced potato, green peas and the remaining ingredients. Sauté for 1-2 minutes and transfer this mixture in a bowl and allow to cool.

2. Stuff well each capsicum with this mixture and cover with the caps and tie individually each capsicum with a kitchen string.

Cooking

1. Take a skewer and skew capsicum leaving a gap of 1 inch. A piece of potato or half cut onion can be used to prevent them from slipping.

2. Roast in a tandoor or over a charcoal grill for 6-8 minutes.

3. Serve hot with choice of salad and chutney.

TO SERVE: 4

COOKING TIME: 6-8 MINUTES

NARGISI SEEKH KEBAB

▼

Ingredients

Boiled potato	-	300 gm
Cottage cheese	-	300 gm
Egg (optional)	-	1 no.
Garlic paste	-	40 gm
Onion (chopped)	-	30 gm
Tomato (chopped)	-	20 gm
Capsicum (chopped)	-	20 gm
Coriander (chopped)	-	20 gm
Carrot (chopped)	-	60 gm
Garlic (chopped)	-	20 gm
Green chilli (chopped)	-	15 gm
Fried mint leaves	-	15 gm
Fried curry leaves	-	15 gm
Sesame seeds	-	60 gm
Salt	-	to taste
White pepper powder	-	1 tbsp
Elaichi javitri powder	-	½ tbsp
Chaat masala	-	1 tbsp
Bread crumbs	-	for binding

Method

1. In a bowl grate boiled potatoes and cottage cheese. Add egg, garlic paste, chopped onions, tomatoes, capsicum, coriander, carrots, garlic, green chilli, fried mint, fried curry leaves, sesame seeds. Mix well.

2. Add salt, white pepper powder, elaichi javitri powder, chaat masala and bread crumbs. Mix thoroughly until it becomes a smooth dough.

3. Divide this mixture into 16 equal portions and make balls.

Cooking

1. Take a skewer, apply the mixture individually along the skewer with a moist palm in a cylindrical shape (4" long).

2. Grill/roast in a moderately hot tandoor or over a charcoal grill for 6-8 minutes.

3. Serve hot with choice of salad and chutney.

TO SERVE: 4

COOKING TIME: 6-8 Minutes

KACCHE KELE KA KEBAB

▼

Ingredients

Raw banana	-	18 nos.
Turmeric powder	-	1 tsp
Salt	-	to taste
Lemon juice	-	1 tbsp
Green chilli (chopped)	-	10 gm
Green coriander (chopped)	-	25 gm
Yellow chilli powder	-	1 tsp
Garam masala	-	½ tsp
Refined oil	-	for frying

Method

1. Peel, roughly slice and parboil the raw banana with salt, turmeric powder and lemon juice. Drain water and cool it.

2. In a processor put bananas and make a fine mince and transfer it to a bowl.

3. Add chopped coriander, green chilli, yellow chilli powder and garam masala and mix thoroughly.

4. Divide the mixture into 16 equal portions and give it a desired shape, either round or banana shape.

Cooking

1. Heat oil in a pan and deep fry until golden brown.

2. Serve hot along with choice of salad and chutney.

TO SERVE: 4

COOKING TIME: 2-3 Minutes

▼

Ingredients

Arbi (yam)	-	900 gm
Salt	-	to taste
Green coriander (chopped)	-	20 gm
Green chilli (chopped)	-	10 gm
Ginger (chopped)	-	15 gm
Ajwain	-	1½ tsp
Turmeric powder	-	½ tsp
Refined oil	-	for frying

Method

1. Wash and boil arbi with salt until half done.

2. Drain water and cool.

3. Peel the arbi and put it in a processor to make a fine mince and transfer it to bowl.

4. Add chopped coriander, green chilli, ginger, ajwain, turmeric powder and mix thoroughly.

5. Divide the mixture into 16 equal portions and make balls. Then press each ball between your palms to give it a medallion (tikki) shape.

Cooking

1. Heat oil in a pan and deep fry until golden brown and crisp.

2. Serve hot with choice of salad and chutney.

TO SERVE: 4

COOKING TIME: 2-3 Minutes

KABULI SEEKH

▼

Ingredients

Kabuli (white) chana	-	600 gm
Paneer	-	100 gm
Potato	-	100 gm
Onion (chopped)	-	100 gm
Green chilli (chopped)	-	15 gm
Coriander (chopped)	-	25 gm
Ginger (chopped)	-	15 gm
Ajwain	-	1 tsp
Salt	-	to taste
Yellow chilli powder	-	1 tsp
Garam masala	-	½ tsp
Chana masala	-	1½ tbsp
Kasoori methi powder	-	½ tsp

Method

1. Clean and boil kabuli chana until ¾ cooked. Drain water and cool.

2. In a processor put boiled chana and make a fine mince and transfer it to a bowl.

3. Grate paneer, potatoes and add it to the minced chana along with remaining ingredients and mix thoroughly.

4. Divide this mixture into 16 equal portions and make balls.

Cooking

1. Take a skewer, apply this mixture on it in a cylindrical shape (4" long) using moist hands and grill over charcoal or tandoor for 6-8 minutes.

2. Serve hot along with choice of salad and chutney.

TO SERVE: 4

COOKING TIME: 6-8 Minutes

KANDHAR KE SEEKH KEBAB

▼

Ingredients

Nutrella (soyabean)	-	600 gm
Paneer	-	200 gm
Ginger (chopped)	-	15 gm
Green chilli (chopped)	-	10 gm
Coriander (chopped)	-	25 gm
Salt	-	to taste
Kashmiri red chilli powder	-	1 tsp
Elaichi javitri powder	-	2 tsp
Egg powder (optional)	-	50 gm
Chana masala	-	1 tsp

Method

1. Boil nutrella beans for 2 minutes. Squeeze excess water and put it in a bowl.

2. Grate paneer, add it to the beans and mix.

3. Add ginger, green chilli, coriander and mix.

4. Add salt, Kashmiri red chilli powder, elaichi javitri powder, egg powder, chana masala, and mix with palm until smooth.

5. Divide the mixture into 16 equal portions and make balls.

Cooking

1. Take a skewer, apply mixture in a cylindrical shape using a moist palm. Grill over charcoal or roast in a tandoor at a moderate temperature for 8-10 minutes.

2. Serve hot along with choice of salad and chutney.

TO SERVE: 4

COOKING TIME: 8-10 Minutes

KALE CHANE KE KEBAB

▼

Ingredients

Dry black gram	-	500 gm
Sprouted black gram	-	100 gm
Cottage cheese	-	200 gm
Coriander (chopped)	-	3 tbsp
Green chilli (chopped)	-	2 tbsp
Ginger (chopped)	-	1 tbsp
Onion (chopped)	-	2 tbsp
Chopped spring onion (green)	-	2 tbsp
Chana masala	-	1 tsp
Amchoor	-	1 tsp
Yellow chilli powder	-	1 tbsp
Black salt	-	to taste
Egg powder/bread crumbs	-	60 gm
Melted butter	-	2 tbsp

Method

1. Clean, wash and soak black gram overnight. Boil and cook black grams, drain water and let it cool.

2. In a bowl mash boiled gram and cottage cheese with the help of your palm. Add chopped coriander, green chilli, ginger, onion, spring onion, chana masala, amchoor, yellow chilli powder, black salt and mix well.

3. Add bread crumbs/egg powder, melted butter and mix thoroughly with an open palm to make a smooth dough.

4. Divide this mixture into 16 equal portions and make balls.

Cooking

1. Take a skewer, apply each ball mixture along the skewer in a cylindrical shape with a moist palm. Put sprouted black gram on top of this mixture.

2. Roast it in a tandoor or over a charcoal grill at a moderate temperature for 7-8 minutes. While cooking baste with melted butter the kebabs.

3. Serve hot along with choice of salad and chutney.

TO SERVE: 4

COOKING TIME: 7-8 Minutes

SEEKH SUBZ BAHAR

▼

Ingredients

Green beans	-	500 gm
Carrots (peeled)	-	150 gm
Green peas (shelled)	-	100 gm
Boiled potatoes	-	100 gm
Green coriander (chopped)	-	20 gm
Green chilli (chopped)	-	5 gm
Salt	-	to taste
Yellow chilli powder	-	1 tsp
Garam masala	-	½ tsp
Elaichi javitri powder	-	a pinch
Bread crumbs	-	50 gm
Khus khus (poppy seeds)	-	100 gm

Method

1. Clean, cut and cook beans, carrots and green peas in boiling water. Drain them and squeeze water with the help of a cloth. Keep aside.

2. Put this in a processor and make a fine mince. Transfer to a bowl.

3. Grate boiled potatoes and add to the mince along with chopped coriander, green chilli, salt, yellow chilli powder, garam masala, elaichi javitri powder, bread crumbs and mix thoroughly.

4. Divide this mixture into 16 equal portions and shape each portion into a ball.

Cooking

1. Take a skewer and apply each portion on it along the skewer cylindrical shape with moist in a palm.

2. Apply khus khus on it and roast in a tandoor or over a charcoal grill at a moderate temperature for 8-10 minutes.

3. Serve hot with choice of salad and chutney.

TO SERVE: 4

COOKING TIME: 8-10 Minutes

KATHAL KA KEBAB

▼

Ingredients

Jackfruit (without skin)	-	900 gm
Chana dal	-	150 gm
Salt	-	to taste
Turmeric powder	-	1 tsp
Cloves	-	3 nos.
Small cardamom	-	4-5 nos.
Big cardamom	-	2 nos.
Green chilli (chopped)	-	15 gm
Coriander (chopped)	-	25 gm
Ginger (chopped)	-	15 gm
Yellow chilli powder	-	1 tsp
Refined oil	-	for frying

Method

1. In boiling water, cook jackfruit with chana dal, salt, turmeric powder, cloves, and cardamom until half done.

2. Drain water, cool and remove excess water with a piece of cloth.

3. Put the boiled jackfruit in a processor and make a fine mince and transfer it to a bowl. Add chopped green chilly, ginger, coriander, yellow chilli powder and mix thoroughly.

4. Divide the mixture into 16 equal portions and shape each into a ball and then press it in between your palms to give it a medallion (tikki) shape.

Cooking

1. Heat oil in a non-stick pan and shallow fry till golden brown on both sides.

2. Serve hot with choice of salad and chutney.

TO SERVE: 4

COOKING TIME: 3-4 Minutes

TANDOORI CHAAT-E-CHAMAN

▼

Ingredients

Pineapple	-	1 no.
Apple	-	2 nos.
Pears	-	2 nos.
Guava	-	2 nos.
Tomato (seedless)	-	2 nos.
Capsicum (seedless)	-	2 nos.
Hung curd	-	200 gm
Ginger garlic paste	-	1 tbsp
Red chilli paste	-	1 tbsp
Salt	-	to taste
Garam masala	-	½ tsp
Kasoori methi powder	-	½ tsp
Refined oil	-	20 ml
Tandoori masla	-	½ tsp

Method

1. Wash, peel and cut pineapple in 1 inch cubes

2. Wash apple, pear, guava and cut them (with skin) into 1-inch cubes and keep aside.

3. Wash and deseed tomato, capsicum and cut them into 4 each (large cubes). Keep aside.

Marination

1. In a bowl mix hung curd, add ginger garlic paste, red chilli paste, salt, garam masala, kasoori methi powder, refined oil and mix thoroughly.

2. Put each fruit into this marinade along with tomato and capsicum. Mix and keep in a refrigerator for 1-1½ hours.

Cooking

1. Take a skewer and skew marinated fruits alternately then roast them in a moderately hot tandoor or over a charcoal grill for 4-6 minutes until tender.

2. Sprinkle tandoor masala powder and serve hot with choice of salad and chutney.

TO SERVE: 4

COOKING TIME: 4-6 Minutes

KHUMB GALOUTI

▼

Ingredients

Fresh mushroom	-	1.2 kg
Turmeric	-	1 tsp
Boiled potato	-	150 gm
Ginger garlic paste	-	1 tsp
Yellow chilli powder	-	1 tsp
Garam masala	-	1 tsp
Salt	-	to taste
Chana powder	-	50 gm
Cloves	-	4-6 nos
Ghee/clarified butter	-	½ tsp
Gulab jal	-	2 drops
Refined oil	-	for shallow frying

Method

1. Cut stems of mushrooms and wash thoroughly.

2. Parboil mushroom with a pinch of turmeric powder. Drain water and squeeze excess water from mushroom with the help of a cloth.

3. Put mushroom in a blender and process it until finely chopped. Transfer it to a bowl.

4. Grate boiled potatoes and add them to chopped mushrooms. Add ginger garlic paste, yellow chilli powder, garam masala, salt, chana powder to it. Mix thoroughly and keep aside in a pot.

5. In a small bowl put 2-3 pieces of burning charcoal and place it in the pot beside the mushroom mixture. Put cloves and pour ghee on the charcoal and immediately cover the pot with a lid for 4-5 minutes so that the mushroom mixture gets a smoky flavour.

6. Open the lid. Remix the mushrooms, sprinkle gulab jal.

7. Divide this mixture into 16 equal portions and make balls. Press each ball between your palms to give it a medallion shape (tikki).

Cooking

1. Heat oil in a non-stick pan and shallow fry till golden brown on both sides (3-4 minutes).

2. Serve hot along with choice of salad and chutney.

TO SERVE: 4

COOKING TIME: 3-4 Minutes

KHUMB SHASHLIK

▼

Ingredients

Fresh mushroom	-	400 gm
Tomatoes	-	100 gm
Capsicum	-	100 gm
Onion	-	100 ml
Hung curd	-	150 gm
Ginger garlic paste	-	10 gm
Salt	-	to taste
Red chilli paste	-	1 tbsp
Garam masala	-	1 tsp
Kasoori methi powder	-	1 tsp
Lemon juice	-	20 ml
Refined oil	-	20 ml

Method

1. Clean and cut stems of mushroom. Wash and keep aside.

2. Cut tomato into 4 pieces, deseed. Cut capsicum into 4 and deseed. Peel and cut onion into 4. Cut large cubes of the above items and keep aside.

Marination

1. In a bowl whisk hung curd, add ginger garlic paste, salt, red chilli paste, garam masala, kasoori methi powder, lemon juice, refined oil and mix well.

2. Put mushroom and all vegetables into this marinade and keep for 30 minutes.

Cooking

1. Take a skewer and skew the mushroom, onion, tomato, and capsicum. Repeat in the same order. Roast over a charcoal grill or in a tandoor at a moderate temperature for 6-8 minutes.

2. Serve hot along with choice of salad and chutney.

TO SERVE: 4

COOKING TIME: 6-8 Minutes

▼

KHUS KE SHAMMI KEBAB

▼

Ingredients

Boiled potatoes	-	I kg
Ginger (chopped)	-	20 gm
Green chillies (chopped)	-	50 gm
Garlic (chopped)	-	15 gm
Khus khus	-	100 gm
Salt	-	to taste
Garam masala	-	10 gm
Yellow chilli powder	-	15 gm
Mint sauce	-	50 ml
Bread crumbs	-	for binding
Refined oil	-	for frying

Method

1. In a bowl grate boiled potatoes, add chopped green chillies, ginger, garlic and 25 gms of khus khus, salt, garam masala, yellow chilly powder, mint sauce, bread crumbs and mix well to form a dough.

2. Divide this mixture into 16 equal portions and make round balls. Press each ball between your palm to give the shape of a medallion (tikki). Dust each piece with remaining khus khus ensuring that it sticks well and all around. Keep aside.

Cooking

1. Heat oil in a pan and deep fry till golden brown and crisp.

2. Serve hot along with choice of salad and chutney.

TO SERVE: 4

COOKING TIME: 2-3 Minutes

BIKANERI SEEKH KEBAB

▼

Ingredients

Bikaneri vadi or dry lentil dumplings	-	500 gm
Refined oil	-	for frying
Grated paneer	-	300 gm
Ginger garlic paste	-	15 gm
Onion (chopped)	-	50 gm
Coriander (chopped)	-	25 gm
Green chilli (chopped)	-	10 gm
Tomato (chopped)	-	25 gm
Capsicum (chopped)	-	25 gm
Salt	-	to taste
Bread crumbs	-	for binding

Method

1. In boiling water blanch vadi, drain water and pat dry.

2. Heat oil in a deep pan, deep fry the blanched vadi and keep aside.

3. With a hammer crush vadi into small pieces and transfer it to a bowl. Add grated paneer, ginger garlic paste, chopped onion, coriander, green chilli, tomato and capsicum, salt and bread crumbs to form a smooth paste.

4. Divide this mixture into 16 equal portions and make balls.

Cooking

1. Take a skewer, apply mixture in a cylindrical shape with a moist palm and grill over charcoal for 6-8 minutes. Baste with oil.

2. Serve hot along with choice of salad and chutney.

TO SERVE: 4

COOKING TIME: 6-8 Minutes

DAHI KE KEBAB

▼

Ingredients

Hung curd	-	1200 gm
Gram flour	-	400 gm
Onion (chopped)	-	100 gm
Green chillies (chopped)	-	20 gm
Coriander (chopped)	-	20 gm
Ginger (chopped)	-	25 gm
Salt	-	to taste
Garam masala	-	1 tbsp
Kasoori methi	-	½ tbsp
Turmeric	-	1 tbsp
Red chilli powder	-	1 tbsp
Refined oil	-	for frying

Method

1. In a bowl take beaten curd/gram flour and mix together.

2. Strain the mixture through a sieve and keep aside.

3. Add chopped onion, green chilli, coriander, ginger, salt, garam masala, kasoori methi, turmeric, red chilli powder and mix together and keep aside.

4. Take a deep vessel, pour all the mixture and sauté it vigorously at a moderate temperature so that the mixture does not stick to the vessel. Remove it. Keep aside when it is thick and sticky. Cool it.

5. Divide this mixture into 16 equal portions and make balls.

6. With the help of a wet palm roll each ball into medallion (tikki) shape.

Cooking

Heat oil in a pan, fry till golden colour and crispy. Serve hot along with choice of salad and chutney.

TO SERVE: 4

COOKING TIME: 5-6 Minutes

▼

LAUKI KI SEEKH

▼

Ingredients

Lauki (white pumpkin)	-	600 gm
Grated cottage cheese	-	300 gm
Onion (chopped)	-	30 gm
Ginger (chopped)	-	20 gm
Carrot (chopped)	-	30 gm
Green chilli (chopped)	-	10 gm
Coriander leaves (chopped)	-	20 gm
Salt	-	to taste
White pepper powder	-	to taste
Kebab chini powder	-	a pinch
Elaichi javitri powder	-	a pinch
Green paste	-	30 gm
Fresh bread crumbs	-	for binding

Method

1. Wash, peel and grate the outer part of pumpkin except the seeds.

2. Par boil grated pumpkin with a pinch of salt until soft. Strain and immediately keep in cold water. When cold, squeeze excess water and put it in a bowl.

3. Add grated cottage cheese, chopped onion, ginger, carrot, green chillies, green coriander and mix well.

4. Add salt, white pepper powder, kebab chini powder, elaichi javitri powder, green paste, fresh bread crumbs and mix thoroughly until it binds together.

5. Divide this mixture into 16 equal portions.

Cooking

1. Take a skewer and apply mixture on it in a cylindrical shape with a moist palm. Grill in tandoor or over a charcoal grill at a moderate temperature for 8-10 minutes.

2. Serve hot with choice of salad and chutney.

TO SERVE: 4

COOKING TIME: 8-10 Minutes

ALOO MOTI TIKKA

▼

Ingredients

Potato	-	8 nos.

Stuffing

Oil/butter	-	80 ml
Whole coriander	-	1 tsp
Shahi jeera	-	1 tsp
Ginger (chopped)	-	10 gm
Coriander (chopped)	-	20 gm
Green chilli (chopped)	-	10 gm
Green peas	-	100 gm
Corn (boiled)	-	50 gm
Chana (boiled)	-	50 gm
Salt	-	to taste
Red chilly powder	-	3 tsp
Chaat masala	-	1 tsp
Garam masala	-	1 tsp
Yellow chilli powder	-	½ tbsp
Chopped dry fruit	-	50 gm
Raisins	-	10 gm

Marination

Hung curd	-	200 ml
Cream	-	50 ml
Ginger garlic paste	-	15 gm
Salt	-	to taste
Red chilli powder	-	2 tbsp
Garam masala	-	1 tsp
Turmeric powder	-	2 tsp
Kasoori methi powder	-	1 tsp
Gram flour	-	30gm
Lemon juice	-	25 ml
Refined oil	-	25 ml

TO SERVE: 4

COOKING TIME: 4-5 Minutes

Method

1. Peel potatoes, cut the tip from one side with a sharp knife and make a hollow at least 1-inch deep. Wash and pat dry with a cloth.

2. Heat oil in a deep vessel and deep fry scooped potatoes on slow flame without colouring them. Keep potatoes upside down on a piece of cloth to remove excess oil.

Stuffing

1. Heat oil in a non-stick pan, add coriander seeds, shahi jeera and let it crackle. Add chopped vegetable, peas, boiled corn, chana, all masalas, dry fruit and saute. Check seasoning and let it cool.

2. Stuff this mixture well in each potato and keep aside.

Marination

1. In a bowl take hung curd, add cream, ginger garlic paste, salt, red chilli powder, garam masala, turmeric powder, kasoori methi powder, gram flour, lemon juice and refined oil. Mix well. Marinate stuffed potatoes in this marinade and leave it for 1-1½ hours.

Cooking

1. Take a skewer and skew each potato one by one leaving a gap of 1 inch.

2. Roast in a tandoor for 3-5 minutes until golden brown.

3. Serve hot along with choice of salad and chutney.

KHUMB KE SEEKH KEBAB

▼

Ingredients

Fresh mushroom	-	400 gm
Boiled potatoes	-	150 gm
Cottage cheese	-	150 gm
Onions (chopped)	-	75 gm
Coriander (chopped)	-	10 gm
Salt	-	to taste
Red chilli powder	-	5 gm
Garam masala	-	5 gm
Chaat masala	-	5 gm
Bread crumbs	-	for binding
Roasted chana powder	-	20 gm
Melted butter	-	for basting

Method

1. Clean, wash and blanch fresh mushrooms in boiling water, drain water and cool.

2. In a processor put mushrooms and chop them finely. Transfer them to a bowl.

3. Grate boiled potatoes, cheese and add it to the minced mushroom. Also add chopped onion, coriander, salt, red chilli powder, garam masala, chaat masala and mix.

4. Add bread crumbs roasted chana powder for binding and mix well to form a smooth dough.

5. Divide this mixture into 16 equal portions and make balls.

Cooking

1. Take a skewer, apply the mixture along it in a cylindrical shape with a moist palm along the skewer.

2. Roast it in a tandoor or grill over charcoal at moderate temperature for 8-10 minutes. During the time of cooking baste with melted butter.

3. Serve hot along with choice of salad and chuntey

TO SERVE: 4

COOKING TIME: 8-10 Minutes

HARA BHARA SHAMMI KEBAB

▼

Ingredients

Boiled carrots	-	250 gm
Boiled beans	-	350 gm
Boiled peas	-	150 gm
Boiled potato	-	100 gm
Bread crumbs	-	for binding
Green chilli (chopped)	-	20 gm
Ginger (chopped)	-	10 gm
Salt	-	to taste
Garam masala	-	1½ tbsp
Elaichi javitri powder	-	½ tsp

Stuffing

Almonds (chopped)	-	50 gm
Cashewnuts (chopped)	-	50 gm
Til	-	for coating
Refined oil	-	for frying

Method

1. Squeeze excess water from boiled vegetables and roughly cut them in slices.

2. In a processor put boiled vegetables and make a fine mince. Transfer this to a bowl. Add all the remaining ingredients in the order listed and bread crumbs and mix well to form a smooth paste.

3. Divide this mixture into 16 equal portions and make balls.

Stuffing

1. Stuff each portion of the above mixture with chopped almonds and cashewnuts by pressing it between your palms and then folding it back to give it a shape of a medallion (tikki).

2. Coat each tikki with til and keep aside.

Cooking

1. Heat oil in a pan and deep fry till golden brown in colour on both the sides.

2. Serve hot with choice of salad and chutney.

TO SERVE: 4

COOKING TIME: 2-3 Minutes

▼

Ingredients

Boiled potato	-	250 gm
Cottage cheese	-	400 gm
Ginger garlic paste	-	5 gm
Onion (chopped)	-	50 gm
Green chilli (chopped)	-	10 gm
Coriander (chopped)	-	25 gm
Grated khoya	-	50 gm
Ground mixed dry fruit	-	40 gm
Salt	-	to taste
White pepper powder	-	2 tsp
Elaichi javitri powder	-	½ tsp
Small cardamom seed	-	8 nos
Kewra water	-	10 ml
Saffron	-	1 tsp
Roasted maida	-	40 gm
Bread crumbs	-	for binding
Chopped tutty fruity	-	100 gm

Method

1. In a bowl peel and grate boiled potatoes and cottage cheese. Add ginger garlic paste, chopped onion, green chilli, coriander, grated khoya, mixed dry fruit and mix well.

2. Add salt, white pepper powder, elaichi javitri powder, cardamom seeds, kewra water, saffron, roasted maida, bread crumbs and mix well to a smooth paste.

3. Divide this mixture into 16 equal portions and make balls.

Cooking

1. Take a skewer, apply the balls along the skewer in a cylindrical shape with a moist palm. Apply chopped tutty fruity on top.

2. Roast in a tandoor or grill over charcoal at a moderate temperature for 6-8 minutes.

3. Serve hot with choice of salad and chutney.

TO SERVE: 4

COOKING TIME: 6-8 Minutes

NADRU KEBAB

▼

Ingredients

Kamal kakri (bhen)	-	800 gm
Boiled potatoes	-	225 gm
Ginger (chopped)	-	25 gm
Green chilli (chopped)	-	50 gm
Coriander (chopped)	-	50 gm
Salt	-	to taste
Yellow chilli powder	-	25 gm
Garam masala	-	10 gm
Elaichi javitri powder	-	3 gm
Bread crumbs	-	for binding
Refined oil	-	for frying
Tandoori masala	-	½ tsp

Method

1. Peel, slice and boil kamal kakri until tender. Drain water and cool it.

2. In a processor put boiled kamal kakri, make a fine mince and transfer to a bowl.

3. Add grated boiled potatoes, chopped ginger, green chilli, coriander and mix.

4. Add salt, yellow chilli powder, garam masala, elaichi javitri powder, bread crumbs and mix well to form a smooth paste.

5. Divide this mixture into 16 equal portions and make balls. Press between your palms giving it the shape of a medallion (tikki).

Cooking

1. Heat oil in a pan and deep fry until golden brown on both sides.

2. Sprinkle tandoori masala on top and serve hot along with choice of salad and chutney.

TO SERVE: 4

COOKING TIME: 2-3 Minutes

Chutneys

▼

Chutneys are an essential part of kebabs. Traditionally, chutneys were ground on a silbatta (grinding stone). Now, of course the electronic era has brought in food processors, blenders, etc. Though these gadgets make the task easier, some of the flavour is lost. Like pickles, chutneys are also an integral part of Indian kebabs. Chutneys complements kebabs, while their pungent taste and contents facilitate digestion.

PUDINA & DHANIA CHUTNEY

▼

Ingredients

Green coriander (chopped)	-	50 gm
Green mint leaves (chopped)	-	20 gm
Green chillies	-	4 nos.
Ginger (chopped)	-	3 gm
Garlic (chopped)	-	5 gm
Lemon juice	-	30 ml
Black salt	-	a pinch
Salt	-	to taste
Water (chilled)	-	As required

YIELD: 200 gm

Method

Put all the ingredients in a blender and make a semi-liquid paste by adding chilled water.

MOOLI DAHI KI CHUTNEY

▼

Ingredients

Grated radish	-	80 gm
Green chilli paste	-	15 gm
Yoghurt (whisked)	-	40 gm
Lemon juice	-	10 ml
Black salt	-	a pinch
Salt	-	to taste

YIELD: 200 gm

Method

Grate radish, sprinkle a little salt and keep aside for about 15 minutes to drain off excess water. Add all the ingredients to the grated radish and serve chilled.

LAHSUN MIRCH KI CHUTNEY

▼

Ingredients

Red chilli (whole)	-	70 gm
Garlic paste	-	30 gm
Lemon juice	-	20 ml
Refined or groundnut oil	-	15 ml
Salt	-	to taste
Water	-	30 ml

Method

Soak the red chillies in hot water for half an hour. Then put them in a blender along with the other ingredients and make a semi-smooth paste. This chutney should be set aside for 3 hours before use.

YIELD: 200 gm

TAMATER CHUTNEY

▼

Ingredients

Tomatoes (chopped)	-	100 gm
Green coriander paste	-	15 gm
Ginger paste	-	10 gm
Garlic paste	-	5 gm
Red chilli paste	-	10 gm
Lemon juice	-	20 ml
Sugar	-	10 gm
Salt	-	to taste

Method

De-skin and de-seed red ripe tomatoes. Chop finely the flesh of the tomatoes only. To this add rest of the ingredients and keep aside for an hour before use.

YIELD: 200 gm

▼

MOONGPHALI KI CHUTNEY

Ingredients

Peanuts (roasted)	-	100 gm
Green chillies	-	10 gm
Lemon juice	-	30 ml
Ginger	-	5 gm
Garlic	-	5 gm
Ground nut oil	-	10 ml
Salt	-	to taste
Water	-	as required

YIELD: 200 gm

Method

Put all the ingredients in a blender and make a paste to a granular consistency by adding water little by little.

TIL CHUTNEY

Ingredients

Sesame seeds (roasted)	-	80 gm
Sesame oil	-	10 ml
Mint leaves	-	30 gm
Green chillies	-	10 gm
Lemon juice	-	40 ml
Tamarind pulp	-	40 gm
Onion (finely chopped)	-	10 gm
Garlic paste	-	5 gm
Ginger paste	-	3 gm
Salt	-	to taste
Water	-	As required

YIELD: 200 gm

Method

Put all the ingredients except onions, in a blender, and make a smooth paste. Add finely chopped onions to the paste before serving.

SARSON CHUTNEY

▼

Ingredients

Mustard powder	-	80 gm
Coarsely ground mustard	-	10 gm
Lemon juice	-	30 ml
Vinegar (malt)	-	20 ml
Salt	-	to taste
Refined oil	-	10 ml
Turmeric powder	-	5 gm
Water	-	as required

YIELD: 200 gm

Method

In a bowl mix all the ingredients except oil. Add oil to the mixture slowly, whisking all the time.

NARIYAL CHUTNEY

▼

Ingredients

Fresh coconut (grated)	-	80 gm
Red chilly paste	-	5 gm
Green chilly paste	-	5 gm
Tamarind pulp	-	10 gm
Lemon juice	-	15 ml
Coriander paste	-	15 gm
Black salt	-	a pinch
Salt	-	to taste

YIELD: 200 gm

Method

Grate fresh coconut and mix rest of the ingredients in a glass bowl and serve.

▼

PUDINA DAHI KI CHUTNEY

▼

Ingredients

Green mint leaves (chopped)	-	50 gm
Green coriander (chopped)	-	20 gm
Curd (whisked)	-	70 gm
Green chilli	-	5 nos.
Ginger (chopped)	-	3 gm
Garlic (chopped)	-	5 gm
Lemon juice	-	10 ml
Sugar	-	5 gm
Black salt	-	a pinch
Salt	-	to taste
Water	-	20 ml

YIELD: 200 gm

Method

Put all the ingredients, except yoghurt, in a blender, add chilled water and grind to a thick paste. Fold this thick paste into whisked curd. Check for seasoning.

PIAZ KI CHUTNEY

▼

Ingredients

Onions	-	250 gm
Groundnut oil	-	75 ml
Urad dal	-	100 gm
Asafoetida	-	a pinch
Tamarind pulp	-	20 gm
Whole red chilli	-	2 nos.
Salt	-	to taste
Ginger	-	10 gm
Garlic	-	5 gm

Tempering

Groundnut oil	-	10 ml
Whole red chilli	-	2 nos.
Mustard seeds	-	3 gm

Preparation

1. Peel, wash and chop onion, keep aside.
2. Pick, wash urad dal and pat dry with a cloth.
3. Dissolve tamarind pulp in water (approx. 30 ml).
4. Peel, wash ginger, garlic and keep aside.

Method

1. Heat oil in a pan, add dal and sauté until light golden in colour.
2. Add asafoetida, slit onion and sauté until pink in colour.
3. Add tamarind pulp, red chillies, sauté, stir for a few second. Remove and cool.
4. Transfer to a blender, add water (50–60 ml approx.) and make a rough paste.
5. Remove and keep in a bowl.

Tempering

1. Heat oil in a pan, add red chillies, stir for a few seconds, add red chillies, mustard seeds, sauté until they begin to crackle.
2. Pour at one go over chutney and mix well.
3. Serve at room temperature.

YIELD: 500 gm

COOKING TIME: 10–12 Minutes

(*Note*: The lentil should not get mashed in blender, as chutney should be crunchy.)

TAMATER PIAZ KI CHUTNEY

▼

Ingredients

Ripe red tomatoes	-	300 gm
Groundnut oil	-	30 ml
Channa dal	-	20 gm
Onions	-	150 gm
Red chilli	-	4 nos.
Turmeric powder	-	5 gm
Asafoetida	-	a pinch
Curry leaves	-	8 nos.
Salt	-	to taste
Red chilli powder	-	3 gm

Tempering

Groundnut oil	-	10 ml
Whole red chilli	-	2 nos.
Mustard seeds	-	3 gm

Preparation

1. Wash and roughly chop tomatoes.

2. Peel, wash and chop onions. Wash lentil and pat dry.

3. Wash curry leaves.

Method

1. Heat oil in a pan, sauté chana dal over medium heat until light brown in colour

2. Add onions and sauté until light pink in colour.

3. Add red chillies, turmeric powder, asafoetida, salt and tomatoes.

4. Cook until tomatoes get mashed. Remove and cool.

5. Transfer above mixture into a blender and make a coarse paste. Transfer to a bowl, add curry leaves.

Tempering

1. Heat oil in a pan, sauté red chillies for a few seconds, add mustard seeds and sauté until it begins to crackle. Mix well with chutney.

2. Serve at room temperature.

YIELD: 500 gm

COOKING TIME: 15 Minutes

DAKSHINI HARI CHUTNEY

▼

Ingredients

Curry leaves	-	200 gm
Fresh coconut grated	-	100 gm
Coriander leaves	-	50 gm
Sesame seeds	-	50 gm
Ginger	-	10 gm
Garlic	-	5 gm
Lemon juice	-	1 tbsp
Raw mango	-	20 gm
Salt	-	to taste

Tempering

Whole red chilli	-	4 nos.
Curry leaves	-	10 nos.
Chana dal	-	20 gm
Groundnut oil	-	20 ml

Preparation

1. Wash curry leaves, coriander leaves and keep aside.

2. Scrape and peel ginger, garlic.

3. Peel raw mango and cut into small pieces.

Method

1. Heat oil in a pan, sauté all the ingredients leaving lemon juice, mango and salt at medium heat for a few seconds.

2. Remove and cool.

3. Transfer it to blender, add raw mango, lemon juice, salt and make a fine paste.

4. Transfer it to a bowl.

Tempering

1. Heat oil in a pan, sauté chana dal, until light golden. Add whole red chilli, curry leaves, sauté for a few seconds.

2. Mix well with the chutney.

3. Serve at room temperature.

YIELD: 500 gm

COOKING TIME: 15 Minutes

▼

Ingredients

Fresh coconut	-	200 gm
Cashewnut	-	200 gm
Green chilli	-	15 gm
Ginger	-	5 gm
Coconut water	-	75 ml

Tempering

Whole red chilli	-	4 nos.
Urad (washed)	-	1 tbsp
Mustard seeds	-	½ tbsp
Curry leaves	-	10 nos.
Groundnut oil	-	10 ml

Preparation

1. Scrape the brown skin and grate coconut.

2. Remove stems, wash, slit and deseed green chillies, scrape and wash ginger. Wash curry leaves.

3. Wash lentil in water and pat dry.

4. Soak cashewnut in water.

Method

Mix green chillies, cashewnuts, ginger with grated coconut and make a fine paste in blender. Remove and keep in glass bowl.

Tempering

1. Heat oil in a pan, add red chillies and stir over medium heat, add urad dal and sauté light brown. Add mustard seeds, curry leaves, sauté till they begin to crackle.

2. Mix tempering with chutney.

3. Serve at room temperature.

YIELD: 500 gm

COOKING TIME: 20 Minutes

AAM KI CHUTNEY

▼

Ingredients

Raw mango	-	1500 gm
Sugar	-	1000 gm
Onion	-	125 gm
Ginger	-	60 gm
Garlic paste	-	25 gm
Red chilli powder	-	1 tbsp
Garam masala	-	1 tbsp
Cinnamon powder	-	½ tsp
White vinegar	-	250 ml
Salt	-	to taste
Raisins	-	125 gm
Melon seeds	-	1 tbsp

Preparation

1. Peel, wash and roughly chop mangoes.

2. Peel, wash and grate onion, scrape and mash ginger, put it in a muslin cloth and squeeze out juice.

3. Mix the above onion and ginger juice with garlic paste.

4. Soak raisins and melon seeds in water.

Method

1. In a thick bottomed pan, put sugar, mangoes and cook over medium heat for 12–15 minutes.

2. Add onion, ginger, garlic juice, red chilli powder, garam masala, cinnamon powder and cook till the mixture attain consistency of jam.

3. Mix white vinegar and salt, cook for 2-3 minutes and remove.

4. Garnish with melon seeds and raisins.

5. Keep in a jar to mature for 2-3 days.

YIELD: 1500 gm

COOKING TIME: 20–25 Minutes

▼

SAUNTH (MEETHI CHUTNEY)

▼

Ingredients

Imli	-	250 gm
Sugar *or* Jaggery	-	300 gm
Red chilli powder	-	30 gm
Fennel powder	-	30 gm
Dry ginger powder	-	25 gm
Jeera powder	-	20 gm
Dhania powder	-	20 gm
Garam masala	-	10 gm
Black salt powder	-	to taste
Water	-	800 ml

Preparation

1. In a bowl soak imli in water for about 2 hours.
2. Boil imli with red chilli powder until mashed. Cool and strain.

Method

1. Add all the remaining ingredients in the order listed to the above imli mixture.
2. Mix well and serve at room temperature

VARIATION IN SAUNTH CHUTNEY

Kele Ki Saunth:	Cut medium slice of ripe banana, add it to chutney.
Angur Ki Saunth:	Fresh grapes added to chutney.
Anar Ki Saunth:	Pomegranate seeds (Fresh) added to saunth chutney.
Aam Ki Saunth:	Small cubes of ripe mango added in saunth chutney.
Khajur Ki Saunth:	Dry khajur first boiled and then deseeded, cut into 4, added to saunth chutney.
Kishmish Ki Saunth:	Soak kishmish in water until it swells, add it to saunth chutney.
Phaldari Saunth:	Cashewnut, kishmish and charmagaz, added in saunth chutney.

YIELD: 1000 ml

COOKING TIME: 1½-2 Hours

Rotis (Breads)

▼

Bread is a generous gift of nature, a food that can be replaced by no other.... It is suited to every time of the day, every age of life, and every temperament. It is so perfectly adapted to man that we turn our heads to it almost as soon as we are born and never tire of it to the hour of death. Breads is one factor that unites man! Every where, in every country, every city and every home bread is.prepared and eaten in one way or another.

Not the least of the pleasure breads is its variety. Breads as most people know, is a dough of wheat flour and water, seasoned with a little salt, leavened or unleavened.

In India there is a large variety of breads mostly unleaveaned, prepared in different ways, i.e., tandoori, deep fried, baked and shallow fried. Breads are unleavened and made with wheat flour, maize flour (Makki Atta), millet (Jawar), and milo (Bajra).

In Northern and Central India wheat is the most popular gram and consequently people eat rotis in preference to rice. It is in fact easier and quickest to make Indian rotis than to make bread in the Wastern style.

Glossary

Sift	: Sieving process used for all flour.
Knead	: Kneading is the important process for making rotis (breads). It involves the motion of both hands. The dough is first pushed with the palm and then folded over with fingers. This process gives AIR to the dough and makes it lighter. Kneading helps to distribute ingredients and alternates the protien glutens in the wheat flour. When kneading one should not pour all the water at one go on the flour. To avoid lumps instead sprinkle a little at a time and kneading simultaneously to blend flour and water.
Dough	: It is a blend of flour and water kneaded till soft and pliable. A well-kneaded dough should be non-sticky.
Leavening Agents	: Those substances that help the dough to rise. Usually baking powder, soda bicarbonate, eggs and yoghurt.
Khamir	: Soured dough used for leavening other breads (khamir roti).
Flour	: This dry flour is used while flattening, rolling the dough or dusting the surface. It prevents the wet dough from sticking to the hands.
Finishing	: Apply butter or ghee in the bread, usually after the bread is baked while it is still hot. Even in the methods of making Indian breads, there is great variety.
Tandoor	: For making roti, naan, parantha, khasta, missi. Moderate temperate of Tandoor for baking bread (275°c-300°c).
Concave Tawa/ Griddle Plate	: Phulkha, tawa parantha, makki roti, bajre ki roti.
Kadhai	: For frying pooris, bhatura, kachori, etc.
Conventional Oven	: To bake bakarkhani, sheermal etc.

TANDOORI PANEER KULCHA

▼

Ingredients

Naan dough - 450 gm

Stuffing

Paneer	-	160 gm
Green chilli (chopped)	-	20 gm
Coriander (chopped)	-	25 gm
Salt	-	to taste
White pepper powder	-	I tsp
Shahi jeera	-	I tsp
Melted butter	-	40 gm

Method

Stuffing

1. In a bowl grate paneer and add rest of the ingredients except melted butter in the order listed. Mix well. Adjust seasoning and divide into 4 equal portions.

2. Divide the naan dough into 4 equal portions and make balls. Place the ball on a lightly floured surface.

3. Slightly flatten the ball. Place a portion of paneer filling in the middle, infold the filling and pinch excess dough to seal the edges. Cover with cloth for 5 minutes.

4. Flatten each ball between the palm and make a round disc (8-9" in diameter).

Cooking

1. Place disc on a *gaddi* (cushioned pad) and stick inside a moderately hot tandoor and bake for 2-4 minutes.

2. Remove, apply melted butter and serve hot.

YIELD: 4 Pieces

COOKING TIME: 2-3 Minutes

▼

ROGANI KULCHA

▼

Ingredients

Refined flour	-	500 gm
Salt	-	a pinch
Egg	-	1 no.
Baking powder	-	½ tsp
Sugar	-	1 tsp
Milk	-	50 ml
Water	-	as required
Refined oil	-	20 ml

For Rogan

Refined oil	-	30 ml
Red chilli powder	-	1 tbsp
Egg	-	1 no.

Method

1. Sieve the flour with salt into a *paraat*.

2. In a bowl break the egg, add baking powder, sugar, milk and whisk it.

3. Make a bay in the sieved flour, add the egg mixture and start mixing gradually. Add water to knead a soft dough. Keep aside for 10 minutes.

4. Add refined oil, knead and punch the dough, cover with a moist cloth and keep aside for 2 hours to allow the dough to rise.

5. Divide the dough into 8 equal portions and make balls. Keep aside.

6. Heat oil in a pan, add red chillies to it and keep it for ½ hours. Strain and cool. Add egg and mix it. Add egg and mix it.

Cooking

1. Flatten each ball between your palm and make a round disc. Place it on a *gaddi* (cushioned pad) and stick it inside the tandoor and bake for 2-3 minutes.

2. Apply rogan on the kulcha.

3. Serve hot.

YIELD: 8 Pieces

COOKING TIME: 2-3 Minutes

▼

Ingredients

Naan dough   -   450 gm

Stuffing

Onion (chopped)	-	150 gm
Green chilli (chopped)	-	15 gm
Coriander (chopped)	-	25 gm
Salt	-	to taste
Shahi jeera	-	1 tsp
Melted butter	-	40 gm

Method

Stuffing

1. In a bowl mix chopped onion, green chilli, coriander, salt and shahi jeera.

2. Divide the naan dough into 4 equal portions and make balls. Place the ball on a lightly floured surface.

3. Slightly flatten the ball. Place a portion of onion filling in the middle, infold the filling and pinch off excess dough to seal the edges. Cover with cloth for 5 minutes.

4. Flatten each ball between the palms and make a round disc (8-9" diameter).

Cooking

1. Place disc on a padded cloth and stick inside a moderately hot tandoor. Bake for 2-3 minutes.

2. Remove, apply melted butter and serve hot.

YIELD: 4 Pieces

COOKING TIME: 2-3 Minutes

TANDOORI KEEMA KULCHA

▼

Ingredients

Naan dough	-	450 gm

Filling

Lamb mince	-	150 gm
Ghee	-	50 gm
Ginger garlic paste	-	15 gm
Red chilli powder	-	5 gm
Green chilli (chopped)	-	10 gm
Tomatoes (chopped)	-	75 gm
Coriander (chopped)	-	10 gm
Salt	-	to taste
Melted butter	-	40 gm

Method

Filling

1. Heat ghee in a *kadai*, add ginger garlic paste and red chilli powder, sauté over medium heat for 30 seconds.

2. Add green chillies, tomatoes, salt and sauté until the fat leaves the masala.

3. Add the lamb mince and sauté over slow heat until cooked and dry. Sprinkle coriander leaves and stir. Adjust seasoning, cool and keep aside.

4. Divide the naan dough into 4 equal portions and make balls. Place the ball on a lightly floured surface.

5. Slightly flatten the ball. Place a portion of lamb mince filling in the middle, infold the filling and pinch off excess dough to seal the edges. Cover with cloth for 5 minutes.

6. Flatten each ball between the palms and make a round disc (8-9" diameter).

Cooking

1. Place disc on a *gaddi* (cushioned pad) and stick inside a moderately hot tandoor and bake for 2-4 minutes.

2. Remove, apply melted butter and serve hot.

YIELD: 4 Pieces

COOKING TIME: 2-3 Minutes

NAAN

▼

Ingredients

Refined flour	-	500 gm
Salt	-	a pinch
Egg	-	1 no.
Baking powder	-	½ tsp
Sugar	-	1 tsp
Milk	-	50 ml
Water	-	as required
Refined oil	-	20 ml
Kalonji	-	½ tsp
Fennel seeds	-	1 tsp

Method

1. Sieve the flour with salt into a *paraat*.

2. In a bowl break the egg, add baking powder, sugar, milk and whisk it.

3. Make a bay in the sieved flour, add the egg mixture and start mixing gradually. Add or pour a little water, knead to make a soft dough. Keep aside for 10 minutes.

4. Add refined oil, knead and punch the dough, cover with a moist cloth and keep aside for 2 hours to allow the dough to rise.

5. Divide the dough into 8 equal portions as balls and place on a floured surface.

6. Apply kalonji and fennel seeds and flatten the ball slightly and keep it for 5 minutes.

7. Flatten each ball between your palms and make a round disc. Stretch on one side to give the shape of an elongated oval.

Cooking

Place the naan on a *gaddi* (cushioned pad) and stick it inside a moderate hot tandoor. Bake for 2-3 minutes and serve hot.

YIELD: 8 Pieces

COOKING TIME: 1-2 Minutes

KHURMI NAAN

▼

Ingredients

Naan dough	-	800 gm
Tomato puree	-	300 gm
Salt	-	to taste
Sugar	-	25 gm
Red chilli powder	-	a little
Grated processed cheese	-	100 gm

Method

Divide the dough into 8 equal portions and make balls. Place the ball on a floured surface.

Coating

1. Heat pan, add tomato puree and cook for 5-8 minutes or till reduced. Add salt, sugar, red chilli powder and reduce until thick.

2. Remove from fire, add grated cheese, mix and cool.

3. Flatten the ball slightly. Apply a portion of the above mixture proportionately.

4. Flatten each ball between your palms and make a round disc and stretch on one side in the shape of an elongated oval.

Cooking

1. Place the naan on a cushioned pad (*gaddi*) and stick it inside a moderately hot tandoor. Bake for 2-3 minutes.

2. Remove and serve hot.

YIELD: 8 Pieces

COOKING TIME: 2-3 Minutes

LAHSUNI NAAN

▼

Ingredients

Refined flour	-	500 gm
Salt	-	a pinch
Egg	-	1 no.
Baking powder	-	½ tsp
Sugar	-	1 tsp
Milk	-	50 ml
Water	-	as required
Refined oil	-	20 ml
Garlic (chopped)	-	200 gm

Method

1. Sieve the flour with salt into a *paraat*.

2. In a bowl break the egg, add baking powder, sugar, soda bicarb, milk and whisk it.

3. Make a bay in the sieved flour, add the egg mixture and start mixing gradually. Add or pour a little water, knead to make a soft dough. Keep aside for 10 minutes.

4. Add refined oil, knead and punch the dough, cover with a moist cloth and keep aside for 2 hours to allow the dough to rise.

5. Divide the dough into 8 equal portions, make balls and place on a floured surface.

6. Apply chopped garlic and flatten the ball slightly and keep it for 5 minutes.

7. Flatten each ball between your palms and make a round disc and stretch on one side to give the shape of an elongated oval.

Cooking

1. Place the naan on a *gaddi* cushioned pad and stick it inside a moderate hot tandoor. Bake for 2-3 minutes and serve it hot.

YIELD: 8 Pieces

COOKING TIME: 2-3 Minutes

▼

KHASTA ROTI

▼

Ingredients

Semolina	-	400 gm
Maida	-	100 gm
Aniseed	-	½ tsp
Ajwain	-	½ tsp
Milk	-	100 ml
Sugar	-	2 tsp
Salt	-	to taste
Ghee	-	20 ml
Melted butter	-	for garnishing

Method

1. Sieve the maida and semolina in a *paraat*, put aniseed and ajwain in it.

2. Dissolve sugar and salt in milk.

3. Make a bay in the sieved flour. Pour milk and mix it gradually. Knead it to make a dough. Cover with a moist cloth for 10-15 minutes and keep aside.

4. Add melted ghee and mix gradually, kneading it well.

5. Divide the dough into 12 equal portions, make balls, cover and keep aside.

6. Flatten each (ball) with a rolling pin in a round disc. Prick the entire surface with a fork.

7. Place the roti on a cushioned pad (*gaddi*) and stick it inside a moderately hot tandoor and bake until golden brown.

8. Remove and apply melted butter. Serve hot.

YILED: 12 Pieces

COOKING TIME: 2-3 Minutes

BAJRE KI ROTI

▼

Ingredients

Bajre ka atta	-	500 gm
Salt	-	to taste
Water	-	as required
Melted butter	-	80 ml

Method

1. Sieve the atta with salt into a *paraat*.

2. Make a bay in sieved atta, pour water in it and start mixing gradually. When fully mixed, knead to make a soft dough. Cover with a moist cloth and keep aside for 30 minutes.

3. Divide into 8 equal portions, make balls and cover it for 5 minutes.

4. Flatten each ball between the palms to make a round disc, place the roti on a *gaddi* (cushioned pad) and stick inside a tandoor. Bake for 2 minutes. Apply melted butter.

YIELD: 8 Pieces

COOKING TIME: 2-3 Minutes

MISSI ROTI

▼

Ingredients

Besan	-	750 gm
Atta	-	250 gm
Salt	-	to taste
Onion (chopped)	-	200 gm
Ginger (chopped)	-	20 gm
Green chilli (chopped)	-	15 gm
Coriander (chopped)	-	25 gm
Crushed coriander	-	2 tbsp
Crushed anardana	-	2 tbsp
Yellow chilli powder	-	1 tbsp
Turmeric	-	½ tbsp
Mustard oil	-	50 ml
Water	-	as required
Melted butter	-	100 gm

Method

1. Sieve besan and atta with salt in a *paraat*.

2. Add the remaining ingredients in the order listed.

3. Mix and knead to make dough. Cover it with a moist cloth and leave it for 30 minutes.

4. Divide this dough into 15 equal portions and make balls. Place these balls on a floured flat surface.

5. Flatten each ball with a rolling pin in a round disc shape (6" diameter).

Cooking

1. Place it on a *gaddi* (cushioned pad), stick inside a moderately hot tandoor and bake until golden brown for 2-3 minutes.

2. Remove, apply melted butter and serve hot.

YIELD: 15 Pieces

COOKING TIME: 2-3 Minutes

MAKKI KI ROTI

▼

Ingredients

Makki ka atta	-	500 gm
Salt	-	to taste
Water	-	as required
Melted butter	-	100 ml

Method

1. Sieve the atta with salt into a *paraat*.

2. Make a bay in sieved atta, pour water in it and start mixing gradually. When fully mixed, knead to make a soft dough. Cover with a moist cloth and keep aside for 30 minutes.

3. Divide into 8 equal portions, make balls and cover it for 5 minutes.

4. Flatten each ball between the palms to make a round disc, place the roti on a *gaddi* (cushioned pad) and stick inside a tandoor. Bake for 2 minutes. Apply melted butter.

5. Serve hot.

YIELD: 8 Pieces

COOKING TIME: 2-3 Minutes

TANDOORI ROTI

▼

Ingredients

Atta	-	I kg
Salt	-	½ tsp
Water	-	as required

Method

1. Sieve atta into a *paraat*, sprinkle salt.

2. Make a bay in sieved atta, pour water in it and mix gradually to make a soft dough.

3. Cover with a moist cloth and keep aside for 30-40 minutes.

4. Divide this dough in 16-18 equal portions and make balls and place them on a flat tray. Dust it with flour and keep aside for 5-10 minutes.

Cooking

1. Flatten each ball with a moist palm to give a disc shape (6-7" diameter). Place the roti on a *gaddi* (curshioned pad) and stick inside a moderately hot tandoor. Bake for 2 minutes.

2. Serve immediately.

YIELD: 16-18 Pieces

COOKING TIME: I-2 Minutes

ROOMALI ROTI

▼

Ingredients

Atta (whole wheat flour)	-	400 gm
Maida (refined flour)	-	100 gm
Salt	-	to taste
Cold water	-	as required
Wheat flour	-	for dusting

Method

1. Sieve the wheat flour and refined flour with salt. Mix it.

2. Slowly add water and make a soft dough.

3. Keep it covered with a damp cloth for 30 minutes. The dough should be very elastic. Knead well again.

4. Divide this dough into 8-9 equal portions. Shape them into round balls.

5. Roll out each ball into small rounds on a floured *chakla* (wooden surface). Hold this on the back of your palm and circle it twist it in an anti-clockwise direction and swing it. Then again catch it on the back of the palm of the same hand.

6. Keep repeating until diameter of the same becomes about 30 cms.

7. Care should be taken to maintain the round shape and even thickness throughout.

8. These rotis are cooked on the convex side of the griddle, something like an inverted *kadai* or wok, and take just about a minutes to cook.

9. These rotis are folded into quarters or sixes and served hot immediately.

YIELD: 8-9 Pieces

COOKING TIME: 1 Minute

HARI ROOMALI ROTI

▼

Ingredients

Atta (whole wheat flour)	-	400 gm
Maida (refined flour)	-	100 gm
Salt	-	to taste
Spinach puree	-	50 gm
Water	-	as required
Wheat flour	-	for dusting

Method

1. Sieve the wheat flour and refined flour with salt in a *paraat*. Mix it.

2. Add spinach puree, slowly add the water and make a soft dough.

3. Keep it covered with a damp cloth for 30 minutes. The dough should be very elastic. Knead well again.

4. Divide this dough into 8-9 equal portions. Shape them into round balls.

5. Roll out each ball into small rounds on a floured *chakla* (wooden surface). Hold this on the back of your palm and circle it/twist in an anti-clockwise direction and swing it. Then again catch it on the back of the palm of the same hand.

6. Keep repeating until diameter of the same becomes about 30 cms.

7. Care should be taken to maintain the round shape and even thickness throughout.

8. These rotis are cooked on the convex side of the griddle, something like an inverted kadai or wok and take just about a minute to cook.

9. These rotis are folded into quarters or sixes and served hot immediately.

YIELD: 8-9 Pieces

COOKING TIME: 1 Minute

METHI TAWA ROTI

▼

Ingredients

Atta (whole wheat flour)	-	500 gm
Salt	-	to taste
Methi leaves (chopped)	-	150 gm
Green chilli (chopped)	-	20 gm
Water	-	as required
Melted butter	-	50 gm
Wheat flour	-	for dusting

Method

1. Sieve atta with salt in a *paraat*. Put chopped methi leaves, chopped green chilli and mix together.

2. Pour water gradually and mix. Knead to form a dough. Cover with a moist cloth and keep aside for 30 minutes.

3. Divide the dough in 10 equal portions and make balls.

4. Place them on a floured surface. Flatten each ball with a rolling pin into a round disc (6" diameter).

Cooking

1. Heat tawa, place the roti, half cook turning once and cook.

2. Remove and apply melted butter on one side and serve hot immediately.

YIELD: 10 Pieces

COOKING TIME: 1-2 Minutes

BATTI

▼

Ingredients

Atta	-	500 gm
Baking powder	-	5 gm
Salt	-	to taste
Pure ghee	-	380 gm

Method

1. Sieve atta with baking powder and salt into a *paraat*.

2. Make a bay in the centre of the sieved flour, pour water and mix gradually and knead to form a dough. Cover with a moist cloth and leave it for 10 minutes.

3. Add 80 gms of ghee and slowly mix to form a soft dough. Cover and keep aside for 10 minutes.

4. Divide this dough into 16 equal portions and make balls.

5. Flatten this ball with palm to give a disc shape (2-2½" diameter).

Cooking

1. Grease the baking tray, place the disc on it and bake in a moderate heated oven for 15-18 minutes.

2. Remove, depress on one side to crack open the crust, pour the melted ghee with a spoon on it and serve immediately.

YIELD: 15-16 Pieces

COOKING TIME: 15-18 Minutes

POORI

▼

Ingredients

Atta	-	500 gm
Salt	-	a little
Oil	-	for frying

Method

1. Sieve the atta with salt into a *paraat*.

2. Make a bay in the sieved ata, pour water in it, knead to make a dough, cover with a moist cloth and keep aside for 30 minutes. Divide into 20 equal portions, make balls, apply a little oil and cover with a wet cloth and keep aside.

3. Flatten each ball with a rolling pin into round discs (4" diameter).

Cooking

1. Heat oil in a *kadai* and deep fry the pooris until golden brown, turning once to ensure it puffs up.

2. Remove and serve immediately.

YIELD: 20 Pieces

COOKING TIME: 1 Minute

SHEERMAL

▼

Ingredients

Milk	-	1 litre
Cardamom powder	-	½ tsp
Melted fat/ghee	-	700 gm
Sugar	-	1 tsp
Flour	-	1 kg
Honey	-	2 tsp
Desi ghee	-	2 tsp
Kewra water	-	½ tsp
Saffron	-	1 tsp

Method

1. In a bowl put milk, cardamon powder, sugar, melted fat ghee, sugar and mix. Sieve flour and make a bay in the centre. Add milk mix and knead to make a dough. Work out with fingers until the dough acquires a stringy consistency.

2. Let the dough sit with a damp cloth in a cool place for about 1 hour.

3. In a small bowl put desi ghee, kewra water, saffron and milk. Keep aside.

Cooking

1. Divide the dough into 12 equal portions and make balls. Flatten each ball with a rolling pin into discs (6-7" diameter) and prick with a fork.

2. Place it on a greased tray. Bake it in a preheated oven for 2-3 minutes or till golden brown specks appear on the bread. Flip and bake for the same time.

3. Baste with saffron and kewra flavoured milk mixture.

4. Serve hot immediately.

YIELD: 12 Pieces

COOKING TIME: 3-4 Minutes

BAKARKHANI

▼

Ingredients

Flour	-	1 kg
Cardamom powder	-	½ tsp
Milk	-	300 ml
Kewra water	-	½ tsp
Malai (reduced milk)	-	200 gm
Castor sugar	-	1 tbsp
Cashewnut paste	-	25 gm
Ghee/fat	-	750 gm
Saffron soaked in milk	-	1 tsp

Method

1. Sieve flour in a large *paraat*. Make a bay in the centre and add cardamom powder, milk and mix. Prepare a smooth dough and keep aside.

2. Cream malai with sugar and cashewnut paste till smooth.

3. Pour the melted ghee and paste of malai, sugar and cashewnut into the dough and leave it for 10 minutes. With the help of fingers mix the fat into the dough in a circular motion.
(This involves a great deal of expertise and only comes with practice.)

4. While fat is mixed/blended into the dough it should be noted that the dough is not handled much and no swift movements are made with the fingers.
(To test that the dough is prepared, drop a little with your hands. It should fall in threads.)

5. The prepared dough is then kept aside in a cool place for about 1 hour, so that it does not melt.

Cooking

1. Divide dough into 12 equal portions and make balls. Flatten each ball with a rolling pin into a round disc (6-7" diameter). Prick with a fork.

2. Place it in a greased baking tray and bake it in a preheated oven for 2-3 minutes until brown specks appear on the bread. Flip and bake for the same time.

3. Baste with saffron and desi ghee.

4. Remove and serve immediately.

YIELD: 12 Pieces

COOKING TIME: 3-4 Minutes

TAWA PARANTHA

▼

Ingredients

Ata (whole wheat flour)	-	1 kg
Salt	-	to taste
Butter	-	400 gm
Water	-	as required

Method

1. Sieve atta with salt in a *paraat*. Make a bay in the flour. Pour water and mix gradually to make a dough.

2. Cover it with a moist cloth and keep for 10 minutes.

3. Divide this dough in 10-12 equal portions and make balls.

4. Place the balls on a slightly floured surface and roll it in a disc shape (6-7" diameter).

Cooking

1. Place parantha on a heated tawa and half bake, turning over once.

2. Melt 40 gm butter all around and shallow fry on both sides until brown at low fire.

3. Remove and serve hot immediately.

Note: Tawa parantha can be made with the flavour of your choice, i.e.

1. Lal Mirch Parantha: Add crushed whole red chilli approx ½ tsp in a ball.

2. Kali Mirchi Ka Parantha: Add crushed black pepper to the dough (½ tsp per ball).

3. Ajwain Parantha: Add ajwain to the dough (½ tsp per ball).

YIELD: 10-12 pieces

COOKING TIME: 2-3 Minutes

MALABARI PARANTHA

▼

Ingredients

Maida	-	500 gm
Baking powder	-	a pinch
Salt	-	to taste
Egg	-	1 no.
Milk	-	100 ml
Sugar	-	1 tsp
Water	-	as required
Melted butter	-	100 ml

Method

1. Sieve the flour, add baking powder and salt.

2. Whisk egg in a bowl, add milk, sugar and mix well.

3. Make a bay, add egg mixture and start mixing gradually. Add little water if required. Knead to make a soft dough, cover with a moist cloth and keep aside for 1 hour.

4. Divide the dough into 8 equal parts, make balls and place on an oily surface. Apply butter on the balls and keep them for 20-30 minutes.

5. Now roll the dough in a round disc and make it thin like roomali roti by beating it on a smooth surface.

6. Fold the thin *chapati* like a flan and twist it back into the form of a ball. Apply butter and keep aside for 10 minutes.

7. Roll out each portion in a round disc.

Cooking

Heat a non-stick pan, cook the parantha on it by applying butter until light golden brown and serve hot.

YIELD: 8 pieces

COOKING TIME: 2-3 Minutes

▼

TAWA DAL PARANTHA

▼

Ingredients

Ata	-	400 gm
Boiled moong dal	-	200 gm
Salt	-	to taste
Red chilli powder	-	1 tsp
Turmeric	-	1 tsp
Coriander (chopped)	-	15 gm
Onion (chopped)	-	30 gm
Chopped green chilli	-	10 gm
Melted butter	-	200 ml
Water	-	as required

Method

1. Sieve the flour, make a bay, add boiled dal and all the ingredients. Start mixing gradually. Add water if required and knead to make a soft dough, cover it with moist cloth and keep aside for ½ hour.

2. Divide the dough into 8 equal portions.

3. Roll them out to make a round disc (8-9" diameter).

4. Heat a tawa and cook paranthas on it by applying butter. Serve hot.

YIELD: 8 Pieces

COOKING TIME: 2-3 Minutes

PUDINA PARANTHA

▼

Ingredients

Ata	-	500 gm
Salt	-	I tsp
Mint leaves	-	80 gm
Butter	-	3 tbsp

Method

1. Sieve whole wheat flour and salt together. Make a bay in the sieved flour, add water, mix and knead gradually to a stiff dough. Keep it covered with a wet cloth for 20-25 minutes.

2. Dry half the mint leaves on a hot tawa, cool and crush to a powder. Chop the remaining mint leaves.

3. Mix the rest of the mint leaves with the dough.

4. Divide the dough into 8 equal portions. Shape them into balls.

5. Now roll the dough to a medium *chapati* and smear with butter and sprinkle with flour. Fold the *chapati* like a flan and twist it back into the form of a ball. Keep aside for 5 minutes.

6. Roll out each portion into a round disc (5"-7" diameter).

Cooking

1. Place the parantha on a *gaddi* (cushioned pad) with and stick it inside a moderately hot tandoor and bake for 2-3 minutes until light golden brown.

2. Apply melted butter and sprinkle dried pudina leaves on the parantha and crush between your palms.

3. Serve hot.

YIELD: 8 pieces

COOKING TIME: 2-3 Minutes

▼

ALOO KA PARANTHA

▼

Ingredients

Ata dough	-	500 gm
Butter	-	160 gm
Ata	-	for dusting

Filling

Boiled potatoes	-	150 gm
Ginger (chopped)	-	20 gm
Green chillies (chopped)	-	5 gm
Coriander (chopped)	-	10 gm
Pomegranate seeds	-	3 gm
Red chilli powder	-	5 gm
Salt	-	to taste

Method

1. Grate boiled potatoes in a bowl, add chopped ginger, green chilli, coriander, pomegranate seeds, red chilli powder and salt. Mix and keep aside.

2. Divide the dough into 8 equal parts and make balls.

3. Place the balls on a lightly floured surface and flatten each with a rolling pin into a round disc shape approximately 6" in diameter. Take two round discs at a time.

4. Spread a portion of filling in middle of one disc. Place the second disc on top and seal from the sides with the help of fingers.

5. Flatten again with a rolling pin approx 7" in diameter.

Cooking

1. Heat tawa, half bake paranthas, turning over once. For each melt 40 gms of butter and shallow fry until golden brown on both sides.

2. Remove and serve immediately with pickle and yoghurt.

YIELD: 4 pieces

COOKING TIME: 2-3 Minutes

PANEER KA TAWA PARANTHA

▼

Ingredients

Ata dough	-	500 gm
Butter	-	160 gm
Atta	-	to dust

Filling

Cottage cheese	-	160 gm
Green chillies (chopped)	-	5 gm
Coriander (chopped)	-	10 gm
Salt	-	to taste
Shahi jeera	-	a little

Method

1. In a bowl grate cottage cheese, add chopped green chillies, coriander, salt, shahi jeera. Mix and keep aside.

2. Divide the dough into 8 equal parts and make ball.

3. Place the on a lightly floured surface and flatten each ball with a rolling pin into a round disc shape approximately 6" in diameter. Take two round discs at a time.

4. Spread a portion of filling in the middle of one disc. Place the second disc on top and seal from the sides with the help of fingers.

5. Flatten again with a rolling pin approximately 7" in diameter.

Cooking

1. Heat tawa, half bake paranthas, turning over once. For each melt 40 gms of butter and shallow fry until golden brown from both sides.

2. Remove and serve immediately with pickle and yoghurt.

YIELD: 4 pieces

COOKING TIME: 2-3 Minutes

GOBHI KA TAWA PARANTHA

▼

Ingredients

Ata dough	-	500 gm
Butter	-	160 gm
Ata	-	to dust

Filling

Cauliflower	-	250 gm
Green chillies (chopped)	-	5 gm
Coriander (chopped)	-	10 gm
Roasted jeera	-	5 gm
Salt	-	to taste

Method

1. Wash and grate cauliflower in a bowl, add chopped green chillies, coriander, roasted jeera, salt. Mix and keep aside.

2. Divide the dough into 8 equal parts and make balls.

3. Place the balls on a lightly floured surface and flatten each with a rolling pin into a round disc shape approximately 6" in diameter. Take two round discs at a time.

4. Spread a portion of filling in middle of one disc. Place the second disc on top and seal from the sides with the help of fingers.

5. Flatten again with a rolling pin approximately 7" in diameter.

Cooking

1. Heat tawa, half bake paranthas, turning over once. For each melt 40 gms of butter and shallow fry until golden brown on both sides.

2. Remove and serve immediately with pickle and yoghurt.

YIELD: 4 pieces

COOKING TIME: 2-3 Minutes

MOOLI KA TAWA PARANTHA

▼

Ingredients

Ata dough	-	500 gm
Butter	-	160 gm
Ata	-	to dust

Filling

Radish	-	200 gm
Green chilli (chopped)	-	5 gm
Coriander (chopped)	-	10 gm
Crushed peppercorn	-	10 gm
Salt	-	to taste

Method

1. Peel, wash and grate radish in a bowl. Squeeze out excess moisture by using a cloth. Add chopped green chilli, coriander, crushed peppercorn and salt. Mix and keep aside.

2. Divide the dough into 8 equal parts and make balls.

3. Place the balls on a lightly floured surface and flatten each with a rolling pin into a round disc shape approximately 6" in diameter. Take two round discs at a time.

4. Spread a portion of filling in middle of one disc. Place the second disc on top and seal from the sides with the help of fingers.

5. Flatten again with a rolling pin approximately 7" in diameter.

Cooking

1. Heat tawa, half bake paranthas, turning over once. For each melt 40 gms of butter and shallow fry until golden brown on both sides.

2. Remove and serve immediately with pickle and yoghurt.

YIELD: 4 pieces

COOKING TIME: 2-3 Minutes

METHI PARANTHA

▼

Ingredients

Ata	-	400 gm
Gram flour	-	100 gm
Salt	-	to taste
Fenugreek leaves (chopped)	-	150 gm
Red chilli powder	-	1 tsp
Yoghurt	-	50 gm
Oil	-	2 tbsp
Melted butter	-	320 gm

Method

1. Sieve ata and gram flour with salt in a *paraat*. Add red chilli powder, chopped methi leaves, yoghurt and mix well.

2. Add 2 tsp of oil, knead to form a soft dough. Cover it with a moist cloth and keep aside for 20 minutes.

3. Divide dough into 8 equal portions and make balls. Place it on a dusted surface.

4. Flatten each ball with a rolling pin into a round disc (6-7" diameter).

Cooking

1. Heat tawa, place rolled disc on it. Half cook and turn over once. For each melt 40 gms of butter all around and shallow fry until golden brown on both sides.

2. Remove, serve immediately with pickle and yoghurt.

YIELD: 8 pieces

COOKING TIME: 2-3 Minutes

PALAK PARANTHA

▼

Ingredients

Whole wheat flour	-	500 gm
Spinach leaves	-	600 gm
Salt	-	to taste
Green chilli (chopped)	-	25 gm
Anardana	-	2 tsp
Water	-	as required
Butter	-	400 gm

Method

1. Clean, wash, spinach leaves. Boil water and blanch it. Put it cold water immediately.

2. Drain and squeeze spinach.

3. In a blender put spinach leaves and make a fine paste. Transfer to a bowl.

4. Sieve ata with salt in a *paraat*. Add spinach puree, chopped green chilli, anardana. Mix. To make a soft dough water can be added if required. Cover with a moist cloth and leave it for 30 minutes.

5. Divide this dough in 10 equal portions and make balls.

6. Flatten each ball with a rolling pin and make into a round disc (6-7" diameter).

Cooking

1. Heat tawa, place rolled disc on it. Half cook and turn over once. For each melt 40 gms of butter all around and shallow fry until golden brown on both sides.

2. Remove, serve immediately with pickle and yoghurt.

YIELD: 10 pieces

COOKING TIME: 2-3 Minutes

BHATURA

▼

Ingredients

Refined flour	-	500 gm
Semolina	-	100 gm
Baking powder	-	½ tsp
Soda bi-carb	-	a pinch
Salt	-	1 tsp
Yoghurt	-	½ cup
Sugar	-	2 tsp
Water	-	as required
Oil	-	2 tbsp+for frying

Method

1. Take flour, semolina, baking powder, soda bi-carb, salt and pass them through a sieve.

2. Make a bay in the sieved flour. Mix yoghurt, sugar and about a cup of water, pour this mixture in the flour, mix gradually and knead to make a soft dough.

3. Mix 2 tbsp oil with the dough and cover it with a moist cloth. Keep aside for 1 hour.

4. Divide this dough into 16 equal portions, make balls and again cover with a moist cloth and keep aside to ferment for 10 minutes.

Cooking

1. Grease your palm with a little oil and flatten each ball into a round disc (5-6" diameter).

2. Heat oil in *kadai* and deep fry until golden brown on both sides and it puffs up.

3. Strain excess oil and serve hot goes best with Pindi chana.

YIELD: 16 pieces

COOKING TIME: 1 Minute

KHASTA KACHORI

▼

Ingredients

Refined flour	-	500 gm
Salt	-	to taste
Soda bi-carb	-	5 gm
Green chilies (chopped)	-	15 gm
Ginger (chopped)	-	30 gm
Water	-	as required
Split black gram (urad dal)	-	1/3 cup
Cumin powder	-	¼ tsp
Red chilli powder	-	½ tsp
Fennel powder	-	¼ tsp
Asafoetida	-	a pinch
Coriander powder	-	1 tsp
Salt	-	to taste
Sugar	-	½ tsp
Ghee	-	4 tbsp
Refined oil	-	to fry

Method

1. Sieve the flour with salt and baking powder. Add ½ the ghee and rub between your fingers to get bread crumb texture.

2. Pour water, mix and knead to form a soft dough. Cover with a moist cloth and keep aside.

3. Soak urad dal in water for 45 minutes and coarsely grind using little water.

4. Heat oil in a pan and sauté chopped ginger, green chillies and remaining ingredients except sugar and salt. Stir well and add ground dal cook till all moisture is dried.

5. Add sugar, salt and mix well. Remove and keep aside to cool.

6. Divide the dough into 12 equal portions and make balls. Flatten slightly with your palm.

7. Place a little stuffing in the centre and bring the edges together to form a ball, flatten slightly.

Cooking

1. Heat oil in a *kadai* and deep fry on a slow flame until golden brown and crisp.

2. Remove and strain excess oil.

3. Serve hot with tamarind chutney.

TO SERVE: 12

COOKING TIME: 18-20 Minutes

TAFTAN

▼

Ingredients

Milk	-	125 ml
Yeast	-	20 gms
Sugar	-	3½ tbsp
Flour	-	475 gms
Salt	-	2 tsp
Curd	-	3 tbsp
Eggs	-	2 nos.
Oil	-	20 ml
Ghee	-	20 gms
Kalonji	-	1 tbsp

Preperation

1. In a bowl take warm milk, add yeast and sugar. Keep aside till it starts to froth.

2. Sieve flour with salt in a *paraat*. Make a bay in the centre and pour the fermented yeast mixture, curd, slightly beaten eggs and oil. Knead to form a smooth dough of elastic consistency. Keep aside for 6-8 hrs.

Method

1. Punch the dough and divide this dough into 8 equal portions/size.

2. Brush with oil. Again keep aside for 20 minutes.

Cooking

1. Flatten each ball with your palm making it narrow at one end and broad at the other.

2. Brush with ghee. Sprinkle kalonji and bake in a moderately hot oven for 2-3 minutes.

3. Remove and baste with milk and ghee.

   Serve hot.

YIELD: 8 Nos.

COOKING TIME: 2-3 Minutes

VARQI PARANTHA

▼

Ingredients

Flour	-	I kg
Salt	-	½ tbsp
Ghee	-	60 gm
Sugar	-	25 gm
Water	-	for kneading

For Layering

Malai	-	140 gm
Fat	-	225 gm
Flour	-	40 gm
Kewra Essence	-	few drops

Preperation

1. Sieve flour with salt in a paraat, dissolve the sugar in malai, add kewra essence and stir.

2. Knead to form a soft dough. Keep aside for 30-45 minutes.

3. Add two thirds of melted ghee and in corporate gradually. When fully mixed, knead to a soft dough, cover and keep aside for 15 minutes.

4. Place the dough on a lightely floured surface and flatter with a rolling pin into a rectangular shape. Apply one-fourth of the remaining ghee evenly over the rolled out dough, dust with flour, fold are end and then the other to make 3 folds.

5. Cover and refrigerate for 10 minutes. Repeat the process-thrice.

6. Remove from referigerator, place on a floured surface, flatten into rectangle and make discs 5″ diameter with a round cutter.

Cooking

Melt ghee on a heated tawa and shallow fry both sides over low heat until golden.

TO SERVE: 12 Nos.

COOKING TIME: 2-3 Minutes

ULTEY TAWE KA PARANTHA

▼

Ingredients

Flour (maida)	-	500 gm
Salt	-	to taste
Cashewnut paste	-	50 gm
Sugar	-	25 gm
Milk	-	300 ml/1½ cup
Baking powder	-	5 gm
Desi ghee	-	75 ml
Melted ghee	-	50 ml

Preparation

1. Sieve flour and salt in a *paraat*. Make a bay in the centre.

2. Mix together cashewnut paste, sugar, milk, baking powder in a bowl.

3. Pour this mixture in bay and mix.

4. Knead it form a soft and smooth dough.

Method

1. Divide this dough into 7 equal balls and place the balls on a lightly floured surface.

2. Flatten each ball with a rolling pin into round disc approximately (8" in diameter). Apply 5 gm of melted ghee evenly over the disc and dust with flour.

3. Make a radial cut with a knife and starting with one end of the cut, roll the disc firmly into a conical shape.

4. Hold each one between thumb and forefinger, half an inch above the base, and make sirel movements to compress the rest of the cone to make a ball. Keep for 30-40 minutes.

5. Remove, press the ball placed on a lightly floured surface and flatten with a rolling pin into disc (8" in diameter.)

Cooking

1. Place the disc on a preheated ulta tawa, turn once, apply ghee.

2. Press the disc with a dry cloth from all sides until light brown. Apply ghee and remove.

3. Serve hot immediately.

YIELD: 7

COOKING TIME: 4-5 Minutes

▼

THE SPICE OF LIFE

▼

IF VARIETY IS THE SPICE OF LIFE, IT IS SPICES WHICH LEND VARIETY TO FOOD. SPICES ARE AN INTEGRAL PART OF INDIAN CUISINE. IT IS THE NUMEROUS COMBINATIONS OF SPICES WHICH CREATE VARIETY IN DIFFERENT DISHES.

Spices and Herbs

Their use in food is primarily aromatic rather than nutritional. Spices or herbs are used to flavour food which forms the major part of the meal or dish. Spices play important role in Indian cookery. Whole spices have a different taste from ground spices and when the spices are dried by roasting they taste entirely different again. Simple dishes may have just one or two spices whereas more eloborate dishes might have ten or twelve. By adding different spices the entire taste of the dish can be changed. All spices have their own characterstics and they are used in varying proportions to make the correct combination for a particular dish. It is the art of blending, mixing and combination of spices/herbs which ultimately matters and one can create a variety of dishes, each different and distinctive.

The magic of kebabs is in the blending of spices and herbs. It is important to know about each spice, its characterstic use in a particular dish. In this book I have used two types of masalas — dry and wet. Dry can be a simple to exotic blend, wet masala is in the form of a paste.

The following are the commonly used spices and ingredients in preparation of kebabs:

Ginger (Adrak): It is the root of a plant with a hot rich flavour, vital to Indian cooking. It is used ground or chopped for curries, pickles, lentils or beans. It helps to counteract flatulence, aids digestion and is also beneficial in disorders connected with the formation of phlegm. It increases body heat if taken with jaggery in vegetables.

Carom Seeds (Ajwain): Also known as Bishop's weed. Used as a part of batters, masalas and in savoury dishes.

Coriander Seeds (Dhania): Used whole and in the powdered form in curries and vegetables and as a part of garam masala.

Cardamom (Elaichi): There are two varieties of cardamom — brown and green. The former is generally used for savoury food. The latter with its cool scented flavour, is equally welcomed in a curry blend and in puddings. It reduces the air and water elements, increases the appetite, and soothes the mucous membrane. The seeds are very hard and should be pounded before use.

Turmeric (Haldi): It is a bright yellow powder of the ground rhizone used as a colouring and flavouring spice essential for curries and pickles. It has a warm, musty flavour. It helps in drawing out and balancing other flavours. It has strong preservative and medicinal properties. Oriental women also used it as a cosmetic.

Cumin Seeds (Jeera): Used whole or ground, it imparts a spicy, aromatic flavour to curries, pulaos and raitas. Light roasting in a dry pan enhances the aroma.

Mace (Javitri): It is the dried outer shell of a nut, golden yellow in colour. It has a strong nutmeg flavour. Used whole or ground, it imparts a delicious flavour to sweet and savoury dishes.

Nutmeg (Jaifal): It is a thimble-sized and almost egg-shaped kernel of the fruit. The best way to use this spice is by grating it freshly as and when needed. It goes well with egg, meat and spinach. It has digestive properties.

Onion Seeds (Kalonji): Dry onion seeds are used in pickles and as a topping for Naans.

Allspice (Kaba chini): The name Allspice recognises the fact that the berries smell like a blend of cinnamon, cloves and nutmeg. It is an important ingredient for kebabs. It has a long history as a food preservative especially in meat: It is used either whole or ground, preferably freshly ground.

Black Peppercorns (Kali Mirch): Next to chillies, this is the most commonly used spice throughout India. It has a strong pungent, spicy flavour. A digestive spice, rich in vitamin C, it is used in all meat dishes and some fish and vegetable dishes. It is used whole or ground (preferably freshly ground) and gives an extraordinary lift to the simplest of foods.

Saffron (Kesar/Zaffarn): It is the world's most expensive spice. Deep red-orange in colour, the saffron strands are both a colouring and flavouring spice. They have a pervasive and warm bitter-honey flavour. A small pinch is enough to flavour a dish. Specially cultivated in Kashmir, it is an important ingredient in almost all Awadh recipes — sweet or savoury.

Poppy Seeds (Khuskhus): These tiny ivory coloured seeds are used for their scant flavour and nutty texture. They are generally lightly toasted before grinding for use in gravies. This aromatic spice is rich in protein and stimulates appetite. It imparts a softness in the texture to the meat or vegetables with which it is cooked. It is also a sedative and checks diarrhoea.

Kewra/Keora: Keora essence is extracted from the inner leaves and the flower petals of a small kind of palm common to South India. Not only is it used in desserts but also in some meat and rice dishes. It is used to impart a flowery fragrance to a variety of dishes from rice to sweet dishes.

Garlic (Lahsun): Strong in flavour, it is used as a spice for curries. Used chopped or sliced, in whole cloves or ground to a paste, it promotes the success of the other ingredients and is commonly used with ginger. Medically garlic is reputed to aid digestion, reduce high blood pressure, expel catarrh from the chest and acts as an antiseptic. Because of its overpowering flavour and aroma it should be used with discretion.

Chillies (Mirch): There are three varieties of chillies used in Indian cuisine — green chillies, red chillies and yellow chillies. The green chillies are the fresh peppers, rich in vitamin C and add a spicy flavour to the food. They can be used chopped, sliced, crushed or slit lengthways. Red chillies are the hottest of all peppery spices and should be used with caution. They are a necessary ingredients of all Indian kebabs and are most commonly used in the powdered form. The Ayurved recommends it as an aid for digestion and cure for paralysis. Since it aids the saliva and gastric juices, it helps to overcome a weak appetite.

Fenugreek (Methi): It is an aromatic bitter-sweet spice, reddish yellow in colour. Because of its strong flavour it should be used sparingly. Rich in vitamins, iron and protein. In Ayurved it has been prescribed for reducing fevers and intestinal inflammations.

Salt (Namak): Salt is the first of all seasonings and essential to all dishes. It is a vital preservative for food of all kinds.

Pudina (Mint): The aromatic leaves of this herbs are used fresh or dried in chutneys, salads, fruit drinks or as garnish. The strong flavoured leaves have great digestive and cooling properties.

Mustard (Sarson/Rai): These are yellow or black and have a sharp and hot flavour. Rich in manganese and vitamin D.

Vinegar (Sirka): A sour pickling agent and preservative prepared usually from sugarcane and rose apple (Jamun). It alleviates bilious tumours. It acts as a prophylactic against cholera and intestinal infections. Also relieves nausea and vomiting. Contains 39% active acid from the oxidation of alcohol.

Almond (Badam): The world's most sought after nuts. Used extensively in sweetmeats. Rich in iron, fats and proteins. In India it is used in savoury dishes and also as garnish.

Kaju (cashewnut): Rich in proteins and vitamin B and used in sweetmeats and some non vegetarian kebabs and curries.

Raisins (Kishmish): Semi-dried white grapes used as garnish for sweets and kheer and vermicelli. Deep fried and used as garnish for some kormas.

Curd (Dahi): Can be used in chutneys, raitas, as the thickening ingredients for a sauce or as a marinade for kebabs. Then, of course, it is also used for sweets or served on its own as a mild accompaniment to hot curries. Extremely versatile and in constant demand for the recipes throughout this book.

Clarified Butter (Ghee): Highest quality cooking fat, made from butter. Old Sanskrit writings suggest that the consumption of ghee could improve a person's appearance, power of speech mental process and digestion. It was a staple dietary recommendation for wrestlers. Best preferred cooking medium in India. When applied on freshly prepared naans and rotis it enhances the taste and aroma. A cheaper ghee substitute is hydrogenated vegetable oil.

Khoya: Khoya is a granular residue obtained by evaporating fresh milk. It is a popular base for sweetmeats and halwas and adds body and richness to any sweet or savoury dish.

Butter (Mahkhn): A fat made by churning the cream, rich in vitamins A and D and used for making clarified butter (ghee) which is used as a cooking medium.

Cream Cheese (Paneer): Similar to cottage cheese made by curdling the freshly boiled milk by addition of acids, usually lime or vinegar. Rich in vitamins.

BASIC KITCHEN EQUIPMENTS

▼

A KITCHEN FOR KEBAB PREPARATION DOES NOT REQUIRE A VERY SOPHISTICATED SET UP.
IT NEEDS FEW DISTINCT EQUIPMENTS WHICH ARE AS FOLLOWS:

Tandoor: The clay-oven is the most versatile kitchen equipment and plays a prominent part in the preparation of kebabs and Indian breads. The traditional tandoor is a clay oven fired by charcoal. Lately iron gas tandoors have been invented but these are not successful and nothing to match the versalities of clay oven. It is the charcoal aroma which is important. Temperature plays an important part in tandoor cooking. If the temperature is too high the charcoal is moved to one side with the help of a skewer. If the temprature is low then both the openings are shut off.

Tawa: A thick heavy iron griddle plate, slightly concave and used for making Tak-a-Tak kebabs, chapatis and paranthas etc.,

Paraat: A flat, round utensil with a border mostly preferred in brass otherwise in stainless steel. It is used for kneading flour dough for breads.

Chakla Belan: Chakla is a small marble or wooden platform, belan is a rolling pin, usually made of wood. This pair is used for rolling chapatis.

Kadhai: A deep frying pan similar to the Chinese wok. It is either made in brass or iron or stainless steel. Most common in iron.

Degchi/Pateela/Handi: All of these belong to the same family. They are traditionally made from brass or copper. Nowadays stainless steel is also used. A pateela has stright sides and a horizontal rim. The bottom is lightly rounded. A Handi has a neck that is narrower than the base. A Degchi is a bigger version of the Handi.

Pauni: A small perforated frying spoon.

Karchhi: A ladle used for stirring.

Hamam-Dasta: A mortar and pestle, used to pound dry masalas and pastes.

Sigri: An open iron grill.

Lohe Ka Tandoor: It is an iron tandoor, as distinct from the clay tandoor. It has a kind of dome shape. Iron oven used for making most breads served as shermal, taftan, bakerkhani, etc.

And the usual graters, sieves, stainers, knives, lemon squeezers, etc.

GARAM MASALA (KING OF SPICES)

▼

THE WORD LITERALLY MEANS "HOT SPICE" WHICH ENHANCES THE TASTE OF FOOD. THIS IS MOSTLY IN POWDERED FORM. IT IS A BLEND OF MORE THAN ONE SPICE. EACH SPICE HAS A SPECIFIC AND UNIQUE AROMA. IT PLAYS AN IMPORTANT ROLE IN MARINATIONS OF KEBABS AND IN GRAVIES.

Garam masalas are often a chef's own combination of spices. To make any blend/mix it is important be aware of spices and their characteristics. There are many versions of garam masala. Every chef has his own preferred combination. There are basically two types of garam masalas. One is the chilll hot while the other comprises aromatic spices (spices and condiments).

Its prime use in kebabs is during marination and in some kebabs it is sprinkled over after cooking to provide aromatic flavouring at the time of serving.

One often sees some people sprinkling tandoori masala (spice) over kebabs after cooking. I would not advise this as I personally believe that it over-spices the kebabs, kills the specific aroma of meat and makes all kebabs taste alike.

The art of preparing a garam masala involves grinding or powdering a combination of dried spices and condiments. Spices are lightly roasted on a griller or on a slow flame till a subtle aroma emanates. Remove from fire and grind. Sieve finely. If the masala is still moist, dry it and store in an air-tight jar for further use. For the benefit of the reader who may like to prepare garam masala, I have listed ingredients and the method on next page.

Junglee Masala
Ingredients

Whole red chilli	-	500 gm
Whole cumin	-	500 gm
Coriander seeds	-	500 gm

Shahi jeera	-	150 gm
Kebab chini	-	50 gm
Nutmeg	-	100 gm

Method
1. Put all the ingredients in a mortar and pound with a pestle to make a fine powder.
2. Sieve and store in an air-tight, dry container.

Gross Weight :	1800 gm
Yield :	1700 gm

Shenshahi Kebab Masala
Ingredients

Cloves	-	300 gm
Bayleaf	-	250 gm
Kebab chini	-	50 gm

Method
1. Put all the ingredients in a mortar and pound with a pestle to make a fine powder.
2. Sieve and store in an air-tight, dry container.

Gross Weight :	850 gm
Yield :	750 gm

Sugandhit Masala
Ingredients

Javitri	-	200 gm
Cardamom (green)	-	200 gm

Method
1. Put all the ingredients in a mortar and pound with a pestle to make a fine powder.
2. Sieve and store in an air-tight, dry container.

Gross Weight :	400 gm
Yield :	375 gm

▼

Gulabi Masala

Ingredients

Dry rose petals   -   500 gm

Method

1. Clean and slightly dry rose petals to remove excess moisture.
2. Put in a mortar and pound with a pestle to make a fine powder.
3. Sieve and store in an air-tight and dry container.

Gross weight :   500 gm

Yield :   440 gm

Tandoori Masala

(Garam Masala)

Ingredients

Coriander seeds	-	400 gm
Cumin	-	400 gm
Shahi jeera	-	100 gm
Rose petals	-	250 gm
Javitri	-	150 gm
Cinnamon	-	150 gm
Black pepper	-	100 gm
Bayleaf	-	100 gm
Star anise	-	60 gm
Green cardamom	-	30 gm
Black cardamom	-	50 gm
Cloves	-	30 gm
Nutmeg	-	30 gm

Method

1. Clean and slightly dry the aforementioned ingredients to remove excess moisture.
2. Put all the ingredients in a mortar and pound with a pestle to make a fine powder.
3. Sieve and store in an air-tight and dry container.

Gross Weight :   2000 gm

Yield :   1800 gm

MARINADES

▼

IT LITERALLY MEANS A MIXTURE OF VINEGAR, WINE, OIL, SPICES, HERBS, IN WHICH MEAT, FISH AND POULTRY IS SOAKED BEFORE COOKING. IN PARTICULAR IT IS APPLIED TO KEBABS.

The purpose of a marinade is to season the food steeped in it by impregnating it with the flavour of its condiments. It also softens the fibre of meat and enables fish and meat to be kept longer than it is generally possible.

While there is no fixed time allowed for marination, the time factor is important and depends on the following:

- The type of meat, fish or vegetable to be cooked.
- The type of cut/size and texture – whole, tikka, chunks, etc.
- Type of tenderizer being used.

Marinated meat can be kept for 2–3 days in the refrigerator and used when required. The marination should enhance the flavour of what is being cooked, not completely overwhelm the taste of it.

To achieve the best results in tandoori cooking of various kebabs, marination plays an important role, so care must be taken for therein lies the secret of a delicious kebab. Some tips for marination are as follows:

- In hot climate, marinated food should be stored in a refrigerator.
- Do not use aluminum dish to marinate or keep marinated food in.
- The addition of salt during marination needs special attention.
- For whole meat and vegetables, salt is to be added together with the spices in the beginning. As for red meat, salt should not be added with the first marination as the addition of salt releases water and juices from the meat thus making it stringy. Add the salt to red meat twenty minutes before cooking.

- Use freshly ground spices for good results.
- Dry fruits are added to impart a distinctive flavour, richness, softness and texture to kebabs.
- The marinade should be well mixed and should be of coating consistency.
- For better results, food items to be cooked must be steeped in the marinade to ensure proper marinating.

Basic Marinades

These are the basic marinades used for preparing any kind of kebabs, i.e. tandoori/tawa/fried:

Red Marination

Ingredients

Hung curd	-	500 gms
Ginger garlic paste	-	1½ tbsp
Red chilli paste	-	1½ tbsp
Salt	-	to taste
Kasoori methi powder	-	1 tsp
Garam masala	-	1 tsp
Lemon juice	-	15 ml
Refined oil	-	20 ml

Method

1. In a bowl, whisk hung curd, add ginger garlic paste, red chilli paste, salt, kastoori methi powder, garam masala and lemon juice.
2. Mix them thoroughly until smooth paste and add refined oil.

Note: This marination is used for chicken, mutton, paneer shashlik, etc.

Yellow Marination

Ingredients

Hung curd	-	500 gm

Ginger garlic paste	-	1 ½ tbsp
Salt	-	to taste
Yellow chilli powder	-	2 tbsp
Garam masala	-	1 tsp
Mustard oil	-	30 ml
Turmeric	-	1 tsp

Method

1. In a bowl, whisk hung curd, add ginger garlic paste, salt, yellow chilly powder and garam masala, mix them and keep aside.

2. In a pan, heat mustard oil, add turmeric to it and cook for a while. Pour this oil in the above mixture and mix thoroughly to a smooth paste.

Note: This marination is mainly used for prawns, fish, paneer kebabs, etc.

Green Marination

Ingredients

Mint leaves	-	30 gm
Coriander leaves	-	150 gm
Spinach boiled	-	50 gm
Green chillies	-	12 nos.
Hung curd	-	200 gm
Ginger garlic paste	-	1 tbsp
Salt	-	to taste
Yellow chilli powder	-	2 tbsp
Kasoori methi powder	-	1 tsp
Garam masala	-	½ tsp
Mustard oil	-	30 ml

Method

1. Clean, wash mint leaves and coriander paste. In a blender, grind these with boiled spinach and green chilies to a smooth paste.

2. In a bowl, whisk hung curd, add ginger garlic paste, mint leaves, salt, kasoori methi powder, yellow chilli powder and garam masala. Mix thoroughly and add mustard oil.

Note: This marination can be used for chicken, fish and paneer kebabs.

White Marination

Ingredients

Processed cheese	-	150 gm
Egg white	-	1 no.
Cream	-	300 ml
Cashewnut paste	-	75 gm
Ginger garlic paste	-	½ tbsp
Green chilli	-	3 nos.
Coriander roots (chopped)	-	15 gm
Salt	-	to taste
White pepper powder	-	1 tbsp
Elaichi javitri powder	-	a pinch

Method

1. In a *paraat* (flat vessel), grate cheese. Mash it with your palm. Add egg white and mix it with cheese and rub until the cheese dissolves.

2. Add cream gradually in one direction so that it gets blended/mixed in the cheese.

3. Add cashewnut paste, ginger garlic paste and all the remaining ingredients, then mix them thoroughly.

Note: This is a mild yet rich marination used mainly for chicken kebabs.

TENDERIZERS

▼

Taking off from the famous saying that "**history was made when the sausage met the mustard**" one could say that "**history was remade when meat met the tenderizer**".

For cooking meat in the tandoor or charcoal grill only tender meat or the tender part of meat is recommended as the temperature is ranging from 300°C to 325°C.

The principle of all tenderizers depends on the range of acid content and enzymes. These readily dissolve sinews and muscle fibres, hence making the meat tender.

The most commonly used tenderizers are:

1. **Raw Papaya (kaccha papita):** Generally papaya is an oblong melon-like fruit obtained from a fully grown tree and is used in its raw form. The papaya contains a protein digesting enzyme called papain that gives it its tenderizing property.

2. **Kachri (botanical name):** Cucumis Pubescens— Kachri is a wild variety of cucumis.

3. **Raw Pineapple (Ananas):** The active enzyme found in pineapple is bromalein which has a very similar tenderizing action to raw papaya.

4. **Yoghurt (Dahi):** Fresh milk inoculated with the culture of lactobacillus. It is the lactic acid in yoghurt that helps to break down meat fibres and tenders meat soft and succulent when roaste cooked kebabs.

5. **Lemon (Nimbu):** The citric acid contained in this fruit is what causes the tenderizing. Also used on kebabs, especially when freshly squeezed as the finishing touch to cooked.

6. **Vinegar (Sirka):** These are of two types, i.e., white synthetic and malt vinegar. Acetic acid in the vinegar gives it its tenderizing action.

Commercially prepared tenderizers: Although a convenient substitute, there's nothing like the natural tenderizer.

Mechanical tenderizing: Often it is the lamb which is beaten with the wooden or rough side of a butcher knife/chopper, to break the tissues, thus facilitating the tenderizing process.

PASTES

▼

Ginger Paste

Ingredients:

Ginger	-	300 gm
Water	-	50 ml
Yield	-	325 gm

Preparation:

1. Scrape, wash and roughly chop.
2. Put the chopped ginger in a blender, add water and make a fine Paste. Remove and refrigerate.

Garlic Paste

Ingredients:

Peeled garlic	-	250 gm
Water	-	50 ml
Yield	-	275 gm

Preparation:

1. Wash and roughly chop the peeled garlic.
2. Put the chopped garlic in a blender, add 50 ml of water and make a fine paste. Remove and refrigerate.

Cashewnut Paste

Ingredients :

Broken cashewnuts	-	250 gm
Water	-	125 ml
Yield	-	450 gm

Preparation:

1. Soak the broken cashewnuts in water for 20-30 minutes and drain the water.
2. Put soaked cashewnuts in a blender, add 100 ml of water and blend to a paste consistency. Remove and refrigerate.

Hung Curd

Ingredients:

Curd	-	1 kg
Yield	-	600 gm

Preparation:

1. In kebabs, yoghurt is an important ingredient for marination. It should be hung in a muslin cloth for at least 1½ hours before use to drain out extra water/whey.

Boiled Onion Paste

Ingredients:

Onion	-	500 gm
Water	-	for boiling

Preparation:

1. Peel, wash and cut onion in four pieces.
2. In a *handi*, put the onion pieces and add water.
3. Bring to boil and simmer until onions are soft and the liquid has evaporated.
4. Cool, put in a blender and make a fine paste.

Almond Paste

Ingredients:

Almonds	-	250 gm
Toned milk	-	250 ml
Yield	-	475 gm

Preparation:

1. Soak almonds in boiling hot water for 10 minutes. Drain water, peel the skin off.
2. Put peeled almonds in a blender, add milk and blend to paste consistency. Remove and refrigerate.

Poppy Seed Paste

Ingredients:

Poppy seeds	-	250 gm
Water	-	150 ml
Yield	-	375 gm

Preparation:

1. Soak poppy seeds in warm water for 45 minutes and drain.
2. Put seeds in a blender, add water and make a fine paste. Remove and refrigerate.

GLOSSARY

▼

Spices and Condiments

English	Hindi	English	Hindi
Almond	Badaam	Mace	Javitri
Alum	Fitkari	Mango Powder	Amchoor
Aniseed	Saunf	Melon Seeds	Magaz
Asafoetida	Heeng	Mint	Pudina
Bayleaf	Tej Patta	Mustard Oil	Sarson Tel
Bengal Gram	Chana Dal	Mustard Seeds	Rai/Sarson
Black Gram	Kala Chana	Nutmeg	Jaiphal
Black Onion Seeds	Kalonji	Peanut/Groundnut	Moongphali
Cardamom (Large)	Moti Elaichi	Peppercorns	Kali Mirch
Cardamom (Small)	Elaichi	Pinenuts	Chilgoza
Carom Seeds	Ajwain	Pistachio nut	Pista
Cashewnut	Kaju	Pomegranate Seeds	Anar Dana
Chick Peas	Kabuli Chana	Poppy Seeds	Khus Khus
Cinnamon	Dal Chini	Raisins	Kismish
Clarified Butter	Ghee	Red Chilli	Lal Mirch
Clove	Laung	Refined Flour	Maida
Coconut	Nariyal	Rock Salt	Kala Namak
Coriander Seeds	Sukha Dhania	Rose Petals (Dry)	Gulab Pankhuri
Cumin Seeds	Jeera	Rose Water	Gulab Jal
Cumin Seeds (Black)	Shahi Jeera	Saffron	Kesar
Curry Leaves	Kari Patta	Salt	Namak
Dates	Khajur	Sesame Seeds	Til
Dry Dates	Chhuara	Semolina	Suji
Dry Coconut	Khopra	Star Anise	Chakri Phool
Dry Ginger	Saunth	Sugar	Chini/Shakkar
Dry Fenugreek Leaves	Kasoori Methi	Sultana	Munnakka
Fenugreek Seeds	Methi Dana	Sunflower Seeds	Chironji
Gram Flour	Besan	Tamarind	Imli
Jaggery	Gur	Turmeric	Haldi
Lentil	Dal	Vetivier	Kewra
		Vinegar	Sirka

▼

English	Hindi	English	Hindi
Vermicilli	Seviyan	White Peppercorn	Safed Mirch
Walnut	Akhrot	Yellow Chilli	Peeli Mirch
Wheat Flour	Atta	Yoghurt	Dahi

Vegetables

English	Hindi	English	Hindi
Ashgourd	Petha	Ginger	Adrak
Beetroot	Chakunder	Gooseberry	Amla
Bittergourd	Karela	Green Chilli	Hari Mirch
Brinjal	Baingan	Green Onion	Hara Piaz
Broad Beans	Sem	Jackfruit	Kathal
Cabbage	Band Gobhi	Lemon	Nimbu
Capsicum	Simla Mirch	Lettuce	Salad Patta
Carrot	Gajar	Lotus Stem	Kamal Kakri
Cauliflower	Phool Gobhi	Mint	Pudina
Cluster Beans	Govaar Ki Phalli	Mushroom	Khumb
Coconut	Nariyal	Onion	Piaz
Coriander Leaves	Dhania Patta	Plantain	Kela
Corn	Bhutta	Potato	Aloo
Cucumber	Kheera	Pumpkin	Kaddu
Curry Leaves	Kari Patta	Radish	Mooli
Drumsticks	Saijan	Spinach	Palak
Fenugreek	Methi	Sweet Potato	Shakarkandi
Garlic	Lahsun	Turnip	Shalgam
		Yam	Arbi

Meats and Seafood

English	Hindi	English	Hindi
Baby Chicken	Chooza	Kidney	Gurda
Boneless Cubes of Meat	Boti	Leg of Kid Lamb	Raan
Breast	Seena	Liver	Kaleji
Chicken	Murg	Lobster	Lobster
Chops	Champen	Mutton	Gosht
Chicken Wings	Pankhari	Prawn	Jhinga
Drumsticks	Tangri	Sweet Bread	Kapoora
Fish	Machhli	Thigh	Kalmi